CASENOTE LEGAL BRIEFS

TAXATION

Adaptable to courses utilizing **Klein, Bankman,** and **Shaviro's** casebook on Federal Income Taxation

NORMAN S. GOLDENBERG, SENIOR EDITOR
PETER TENEN, MANAGING EDITOR

STAFF WRITERS

RICHARD LOVICH
DAVID TREBILCOCK
JAMES ROSENTHAL
MATT HARDY

ALSO AVAILABLE!
FEDERAL INCOME TAX OUTLINE
This Casenote Legal Briefs volume is now cross-referenced to the new *Casenote Law Outline* on Federal Income Tax by Prof. Joseph Dodge

PUBLISHED BY **CASENOTES PUBLISHING CO., INC. 1640 5th ST., SUITE 208, SANTA MONICA, CA 90401**

ISBN 0-87457-127-8

FORMAT FOR THE CASENOTE LEGAL BRIEF

PARTY ID: Quick identification of the relationship between the parties.

PALSGRAF v. LONG ISLAND R.R. CO.
Injured bystander (P) v. Railroad company (D)
N.Y. Ct. App., 248 N.Y. 339, 162 N.E. 99 (1928).

NATURE OF CASE: This section identifies the form of action (e.g., breach of contract, negligence, battery), the type of proceeding (e.g., demurrer, appeal from trial court's jury instructions) or the relief sought (e.g., damages, injunction, criminal sanctions).

NATURE OF CASE: Appeal from judgment affirming verdict for plaintiff seeking damages for personal injury.

FACT SUMMARY: This is included to refresh the student's memory and can be used as a quick reminder of the facts.

FACT SUMMARY: Helen Palsgraf (P) was injured on R.R.'s (D) train platform when R.R.'s (D) guard helped a passenger aboard a moving train, causing his package to fall on the tracks. The package contained fireworks which exploded, creating a shock that tipped a scale onto Palsgraf (P).

CONCISE RULE OF LAW: Summarizes the general principle of law that the case illustrates. It may be used for instant recall of the court's holding and for classroom discussion or home review.

CONCISE RULE OF LAW: The risk reasonably to be perceived defines the duty to be obeyed.

FACTS: This section contains all relevant facts of the case, including the contentions of the parties and the lower court holdings. It is written in a logical order to give the student a clear understanding of the case. The plaintiff and defendant are identified by their proper names throughout and are always labeled with a (P) or (D).

FACTS: Helen Palsgraf (P) purchased a ticket to Rockaway Beach from R.R. (D) and was waiting on the train platform. As she waited, two men ran to catch a train that was pulling out from the platform. The first man jumped aboard, but the second man, who appeared as if he might fall, was helped aboard by the guard on the train who had kept the door open so they could jump aboard. A guard on the platform also helped by pushing him onto the train. The man was carrying a package wrapped in newspaper. In the process, the man dropped his package, which fell on the tracks. The package contained fireworks and exploded. The shock of the explosion was apparently of great enough strength to tip over some scales at the other end of the platform, which fell on Palsgraf (P) and injured her. A jury awarded her damages, and R.R. (D) appealed.

ISSUE: The issue is a concise question that brings out the essence of the opinion as it relates to the section of the casebook in which the case appears. Both substantive and procedural issues are included if relevant to the decision.

ISSUE: Does the risk reasonably to be perceived define the duty to be obeyed?

HOLDING AND DECISION: This section offers a clear and in-depth discussion of the rule of the case and the court's rationale. It is written in easy-to-understand language and answers the issue(s) presented by applying the law to the facts of the case. When relevant, it includes a thorough discussion of the exceptions to the case as listed by the court, any major cites to other cases on point, and the names of the judges who wrote the decisions.

HOLDING AND DECISION: (Cardozo, C.J.) Yes. The risk reasonably to be perceived defines the duty to be obeyed. If there is no foreseeable hazard to the injured party as the result of a seemingly innocent act, the act does not become a tort because it happened to be a wrong as to another. If the wrong was not willful, the plaintiff must show that the act as to her had such great and apparent possibilities of danger as to entitle her to protection. Negligence in the abstract is not enough upon which to base liability. Negligence is a relative concept, evolving out of the common law doctrine of trespass on the case. To establish liability, the defendant must owe a legal duty of reasonable care to the injured party. A cause of action in tort will lie where harm, though unintended, could have been averted or avoided by observance of such a duty. The scope of the duty is limited by the range of danger that a reasonable person could foresee. In this case, there was nothing to suggest from the appearance of the parcel or otherwise that the parcel contained fireworks. The guard could not reasonably have had any warning of a threat to Palsgraf (P), and R.R. (D) therefore cannot be held liable. Judgment is reversed in favor of R.R. (D).

CONCURRENCE / DISSENT: All concurrences and dissents are briefed whenever they are included by the casebook editor.

DISSENT: (Andrews, J.) The concept that there is no negligence unless R.R. (D) owes a legal duty to take care as to Palsgraf (P) herself is too narrow. Everyone owes to the world at large the duty of refraining from those acts that may unreasonably threaten the safety of others. If the guard's action was negligent as to those nearby, it was also negligent as to those outside what might be termed the "danger zone." For Palsgraf (P) to recover, R.R.'s (D) negligence must have been the proximate cause of her injury, a question of fact for the jury.

EDITOR'S ANALYSIS: This last paragraph gives the student a broad understanding of where the case "fits in" with other cases in the section of the book and with the entire course. It is a hornbook-style discussion indicating whether the case is a majority or minority opinion and comparing the principal case with other cases in the casebook. It may also provide analysis from restatements, uniform codes, and law review articles. The editor's analysis will prove to be invaluable to classroom discussion.

EDITOR'S ANALYSIS: The majority defined the limit of the defendant's liability in terms of the danger that a reasonable person in defendant's situation would have perceived. The dissent argued that the limitation should not be placed on liability, but rather on damages. Judge Andrews suggested that only injuries that would not have happened but for R.R.'s (D) negligence should be compensated. Both the majority and dissent recognized the policy-driven need to limit liability for negligent acts, seeking, in the words of Judge Andrews, to define a framework "that will be practical and in keeping with the general understanding of mankind." The Restatement (Second) of Torts has accepted Judge Cardozo's view..

CROSS-REFERENCE TO OUTLINE: Wherever possible, following each case is a cross-reference linking the subject matter of the issue to the appropriate place in the *Casenote Law Outline*, which provides further information on the subject.

[For more information on foreseeability, see Casenote Law Outline on Torts, Chapter 8, § II. 2., Proximate Cause.]

QUICKNOTES: Conveniently defines legal terms found in the case and summarizes the nature of any statutes, codes, or rules referred to in the text.

QUICKNOTES

FORESEEABILITY - The reasonable anticipation that damage is a likely result from certain acts or omissions.

NEGLIGENCE - Failure to exercise that degree of care which a person of ordinary prudence would exercise under similiar circumstances.

PROXIMATE CAUSE - Something which in natural and continuous sequence, unbroken by any new intervening cause, produces an event, and without which the injury would not have occurred.

NOTE TO STUDENT

OUR GOAL. It is the goal of Casenotes Publishing Company, Inc. to create and distribute the finest, clearest and most accurate legal briefs available. To this end, we are constantly seeking new ideas, comments and constructive criticism. As a user of *Casenote Legal Briefs,* your suggestions will be highly valued. With all correspondence, please include your complete name, address, and telephone number, including area code and zip code.

THE TOTAL STUDY SYSTEM. Casenote Legal Briefs are just one part of the Casenotes TOTAL STUDY SYSTEM. Most briefs are (wherever possible) cross-referenced to the appropriate *Casenote Law Outline,* which will elaborate on the issue at hand. By purchasing a Law Outline together with your Legal Brief, you will have both parts of the Casenotes TOTAL STUDY SYSTEM. (See the advertising in the front of this book for a list of Law Outlines currently available.)

A NOTE ABOUT LANGUAGE. Please note that the language used in *Casenote Legal Briefs* in reference to minority groups and women reflects terminology used within the historical context of the time in which the respective courts wrote the opinions. We at Casenotes Publishing Co., Inc. are well aware of and very sensitive to the desires of all people to be treated with dignity and to be referred to as they prefer. Because such preferences change from time to time, and because the language of the courts reflects the time period in which opinions were written, our case briefs will not necessarily reflect contemporary references. We appreciate your understanding and invite your comments.

A NOTE REGARDING NEW EDITIONS. As of our press date, this Casenote Legal Brief is current and includes briefs of all cases in the current version of the casebook, divided into chapters that correspond to that edition of the casebook. However, occasionally a new edition of the casebook comes out in the interim, and sometimes the casebook author will make changes in the sequence of the cases in the chapters, add or delete cases, or change the chapter titles. Should you be using this Legal Brief in conjuction with a casebook that was issued later than this book, you can receive all of the newer cases, which are available free from us, by sending in the "Supplement Request Form" in this section of the book (please follow all instructions on that form). The Supplement(s) will contain all the missing cases, and will bring your Casenote Legal Brief up to date.

EDITOR'S NOTE. Casenote Legal Briefs are intended to supplement the student's casebook, not replace it. There is no substitute for the student's own mastery of this important learning and study technique. If used properly, *Casenote Legal Briefs* are an effective law study aid that will serve to reinforce the student's understanding of the cases.

SUPPLEMENT REQUEST FORM

At the time this book was printed, a brief was included for every major case in the casebook and for every existing supplement to the casebook. However, if a new supplement to the casebook (or a new edition of the casebook) has been published since this publication was printed and if that casebook supplement (or new edition of the casebook) was available for sale at the time you purchased this Casenote Legal Briefs book, we will be pleased to provide you the new cases contained therein AT NO CHARGE when you send us a stamped, self-addressed envelope.

TO OBTAIN YOUR FREE SUPPLEMENT MATERIAL, **YOU MUST FOLLOW THE INSTRUCTIONS BELOW PRECISELY** OR YOUR REQUEST WILL NOT BE ACKNOWLEDGED!

1. Please check if there is in fact an existing supplement and, if so, that the cases are not already included in your Casenote Legal Briefs. Check the main table of cases as well as the supplement table of cases, if any.

2. **REMOVE THIS ENTIRE PAGE FROM THE BOOK.** You MUST send this ORIGINAL page to receive your supplement. This page acts as your proof of purchase and contains the reference number necessary to fill your supplement request properly. No photocopy of this page or written request will be honored or answered. Any request from which the reference number has been removed, altered or obliterated will not be honored.

3. Prepare a STAMPED self-addressed envelope for return mailing. Be sure to use a FULL SIZE (9 X 12) ENVELOPE (MANILA TYPE) so that the supplement will fit and AFFIX ENOUGH POSTAGE TO COVER 3 OZ. **ANY SUPPLEMENT REQUEST NOT ACCOMPANIED BY A STAMPED SELF-ADDRESSED ENVELOPE WILL ABSOLUTELY NOT BE FILLED OR ACKNOWLEDGED.**

4. MULTIPLE SUPPLEMENT REQUESTS: If you are ordering more than one supplement, we suggest that you enclose a stamped, self-addressed envelope for each supplement requested. If you enclose only one envelope for a multiple request, your order may not be filled immediately should any supplement which you requested still be in production. In other words, your order will be held by us until it can be filled completely.

5. Casenotes prints two kinds of supplements. A "New Edition" supplement is issued when a new edition of your casebook is published. A "New Edition" supplement gives you all major cases found in the new edition of the casebook which did not appear in the previous edition. A regular "supplement" is issued when a paperback supplement to your casebook is published. If the box at the lower right is stamped, then the "New Edition" supplement was provided to your bookstore and is *not* available from Casenotes; however, Casenotes will still send you any regular "supplements" which have been printed either before or after the new edition of your casebook appeared and which, according to the reference number at the top of this page, have not been included in this book. If the box is not stamped, Casenotes will send you any supplements, "New Edition" and/or regular, needed to completely update your Casenote Legal Briefs.

NOTE: REQUESTS FOR SUPPLEMENTS WILL NOT BE FILLED UNLESS THESE INSTRUCTIONS ARE COMPLIED WITH!

6. Fill in the following information:

    Full title of CASEBOOK _____ **TAXATION**_____

    CASEBOOK author's name _____ **Klein, Bankman and Shaviro**_____

    Copyright year of new edition or new paperback supplement

    Name and location of bookstore where this Casenote Legal Brief was purchased _____

    Name and location of law school you attend _____

    Any comments regarding Casenote Legal Briefs _____

    NOTE: IF THIS BOX IS STAMPED, NO NEW EDITION SUPPLEMENT CAN BE OBTAINED BY MAIL.

PUBLISHED BY CASENOTES PUBLISHING CO., INC. 1640 5th ST, SUITE 208 SANTA MONICA, CA 90401

PLEASE PRINT

NAME _____ PHONE _____ DATE _____

ADDRESS/CITY/STATE/ZIP _____

Totally free access to briefs online!

Download the cases you want to include in your notes or outlines with full cut and paste abilities. Please fill out this form to be given access. No photocopies of this form will be accepted.

① **Name:** _____ **Phone:** (____) _____

    Address: _____ **Apt.:**_____

    City: _____ **State:**_____ **Zip Code:** _____

    Law School: _____ **Year (circle one):**   1st   2nd   3rd

② **Cut out the UPC found on the lower left hand corner on the back cover of this book. Staple the UPC inside this box. Only the original UPC from this book will be accepted. (No photocopies or store stickers are allowed.)**

> **Attach UPC inside this box.**

③ **E-mail:** _____ **(Print LEGIBLY or you may not get access!)**

④ **Title (course subject) of this book:** _____

⑤ **Adaptable to which casebook author:** _____

⑥ **Mail the completed form to:**   Casenote Online Access
                                   1640 Fifth Street, Suite 208
                                   Santa Monica, CA 90401

I understand that online access is granted solely to the purchaser of this book for the academic year in which it was purchased. Any other usage is not authorized and will result in immediate termination of access. Sharing of codes is strictly prohibited.

_____
Signature

Upon receipt of this completed form, you will be e-mailed codes so that you may access the briefs found in this book at **www.casenotes.com**.

Announcing the First *Totally Integrated* Law Study System

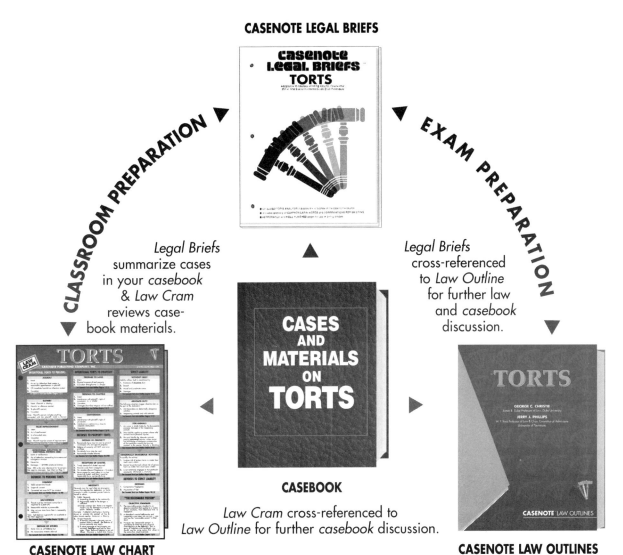

CASENOTE LEGAL BRIEFS

CLASSROOM PREPARATION

EXAM PREPARATION

Legal Briefs summarize cases in your *casebook* & *Law Cram* reviews case-book materials.

Legal Briefs cross-referenced to *Law Outline* for further law and *casebook* discussion.

CASEBOOK

Law Cram cross-referenced to *Law Outline* for further *casebook* discussion.

CASENOTE LAW CHART

CASENOTE LAW OUTLINES

PERIODIC REVIEWS

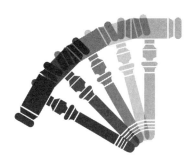

CASENOTES PUBLISHING COMPANY INC.

"Preparation is nine-tenths of the law..."

the Ultimate Outlin

➤ *RENOWNED AUTHORS: Every **Casenote Law Outline** is written by highly respected, nationally recognized professors.*

➤ *KEYED TO **CASENOTE LEGAL BRIEF** BOOKS: In most cases, **Casenote Law Outlines** work in conjunction with the **Casenote Legal Briefs** so that you can see how each case in your textbook relates to the entire subject area. In addition, **Casenote Law Outlines** are cross-referenced to most major casebooks.*

➤ *FREE SUPPLEMENT SERVICE: As part of being the most up-to-date legal outline on the market, whenever a new supplement is published, the corresponding outline can be updated for free using the supplement request form found in this book.*

ADMINISTRATIVE LAW (1999) **$21.95**
   Charles H. Koch, Jr., Dudley W. Woodbridge Professor of Law, College of William and Mary
   Sidney A. Shapiro, John M. Rounds Professor of Law, University of Kansas

CIVIL PROCEDURE (1999) **$22.95**
   John B. Oakley, Professor of Law, University of California, Davis School of Law
   Rex R. Perschbacher, Professor and Dean of University of California, Davis School of Law

COMMERCIAL LAW (see SALES ● SECURED TRANSACTIONS ● NEGOTIABLE INSTRUMENTS & PAYMENT SYSTEMS)

CONFLICT OF LAWS (1996) **$21.95**
   Luther L. McDougal, III, W.R. Irby Professor of Law, Tulane University
   Robert L. Felix, James P. Mozingo, III, Professor of Law, University of South Carolina

CONSTITUTIONAL LAW (1997) **$24.95**
   Gary Goodpaster, Professor of Law, University of California, Davis School of Law

CONTRACTS (1999) **$21.95**
   Daniel Wm. Fessler, Professor of Law, University of California, Davis School of Law

CORPORATIONS (2000) **$24.95**
   Lewis D. Solomon, Arthur Selwin Miller Research Professor of Law, George Washington University
   Daniel Wm. Fessler, Professor of Law, University of California, Davis School of Law
   Arthur E. Wilmarth, Jr., Associate Professor of Law, George Washington University

CRIMINAL LAW (1999) **$21.95**
   Joshua Dressler, Professor of Law, McGeorge School of Law

CRIMINAL PROCEDURE (1999) **$20.95**
   Joshua Dressler, Professor of Law, McGeorge School of Law

ESTATE & GIFT TAX (2000) **$22.95**
   Joseph M. Dodge, W.H. Francis Professor of Law, University of Texas at Austin

EVIDENCE (1996) **$23.95**
   Kenneth Graham, Jr., Professor of Law, University of California, Los Angeles School of Law

FEDERAL COURTS (1997) **$22.95**
   Howard P. Fink, Isadore and Ida Topper Professor of Law, Ohio State University
   Linda S. Mullenix, Bernard J. Ward Centennial Professor of Law, University of Texas

FEDERAL INCOME TAXATION (1998) **$22.95**
   Joseph M. Dodge, W.H. Francis Professor of Law, University of Texas at Austin

LEGAL RESEARCH (1996) **$21.95**
   Nancy L. Schultz, Professor of Law, Chapman University
   Louis J. Sirico, Jr., Professor of Law, Villanova University

NEGOTIABLE INSTRUMENTS & PAYMENT SYSTEMS (1995) **$22.95**
   Donald B. King, Professor of Law, Saint Louis University
   Peter Winship, James Cleo Thompson, Sr. Trustee Professor, SMU

PROPERTY (1999) **$22.95**
   Sheldon F. Kurtz, Percy Bordwell Professor of Law, University of Iowa
   Patricia Cain, Professor of Law, University of Iowa

SALES (2000) **$22.95**
   Robert E. Scott, Dean and Lewis F. Powell, Jr. Professor of Law, University of Virginia
   Donald B. King, Professor of Law, Saint Louis University

SECURED TRANSACTIONS (1995 w/ '96 supp.) **$20.95**
   Donald B. King, Professor of Law, Saint Louis University

TORTS (1999) **$22.95**
   George C. Christie, James B. Duke Professor of Law, Duke University
   Jerry J. Phillips, W.P. Toms Professor of Law, University of Tennessee

WILLS, TRUSTS, & ESTATES (1996) **$22.95**
   William M. McGovern, Professor of Law, University of California, Los Angeles School of Law

CASENOTE LEGAL BRIEFS

PRICE LIST — EFFECTIVE JULY 1, 2000 ● PRICES SUBJECT TO CHANGE WITHOUT NOTICE

Ref. No.	Course	Adaptable to Courses Utilizing	Retail Price
1265	ADMINISTRATIVE LAW	ASIMOW, BONFIELD & LEVIN	21.00
1263	ADMINISTRATIVE LAW	BREYER, STEWART & SUNSTEIN	22.00
1266	ADMINISTRATIVE LAW	CASS, DIVER & BEERMAN	20.00
1260	ADMINISTRATIVE LAW	GELLHORN, B., S., R. & F.	20.00
1268	ADMINISTRATIVE LAW	FUNK, SHAPIRO & WEAVER	22.00
1264	ADMINISTRATIVE LAW	MASHAW, MERRILL & SHANE	21.50
1267	ADMINISTRATIVE LAW	REESE	22.00
1262	ADMINISTRATIVE LAW	SCHWARTZ	21.00
1350	AGENCY & PARTNERSHIP (ENT.ORG)	CONARD, KNAUSS & SIEGEL	24.00
1351	AGENCY & PARTNERSHIP	HYNES	24.00
1281	ANTITRUST (TRADE REGULATION)	HANDLER, P., G. & W.	20.50
1283	ANTITRUST	SULLIVAN & HOVENKAMP	21.00
1611	BANKING LAW	MACEY & MILLER	20.00
1305	BANKRUPTCY	JORDAN, WARREN & BUSSELL	20.00
1058	BUSINESS ASSOCIATIONS (CORPORATIONS)	KLEIN, RAMSEYER & BAINBRIDGE	22.00
1059	BUSINESS ORGANIZATIONS (CORPORATIONS)	SODERQUIST, S., C., & S.	24.00
1040	CIVIL PROCEDURE	COUND, F., M. & S	21.00
1043	CIVIL PROCEDURE	FIELD, KAPLAN & CLERMONT	23.00
1049	CIVIL PROCEDURE	FREER & PERDUE	19.00
1041	CIVIL PROCEDURE	HAZARD, TAIT & FLETCHER	22.00
1047	CIVIL PROCEDURE	MARCUS, REDISH & SHERMAN	22.00
1044	CIVIL PROCEDURE	ROSENBERG, S. & D.	23.00
1046	CIVIL PROCEDURE	YEAZELL	20.00
1311	COMM'L LAW	FARNSWORTH, H., R., H. & M.	22.00
1312	COMM'L LAW	JORDAN, WARREN & WALT	22.00
1310	COMM'L LAW (SALES/SEC.TR./PAY.LAW [Sys.])	SPEIDEL, SUMMERS & WHITE	24.00
1313	COMM'L LAW (SALES/SEC.TR./PAY.LAW)	WHALEY	23.00
1314	COMMERCIAL TRANSACTIONS	LOPUKI, W., K. & M.	22.00
1320	COMMUNITY PROPERTY	BIRD	20.50
1630	COMPARATIVE LAW	SCHLESINGER, B., D., H.& W.	19.00
1048	COMPLEX LITIGATION	MARCUS & SHERMAN	20.00
1072	CONFLICTS	BRILMAYER	20.00
1071	CONFLICTS	CRAMTON, C.K., & K.	20.00
1070	CONFLICTS	HAY, WEINTRAUB & BORCHER	23.00
1073	CONFLICTS	SYMEONIDES, P., & M.	23.00
1086	CONSTITUTIONAL LAW	BREST, LEVINSON, B.& A.	21.00
1082	CONSTITUTIONAL LAW	COHEN & VARAT	24.00
1088	CONSTITUTIONAL LAW	FARBER, ESKRIDGE & FRICKEY	21.00
1080	CONSTITUTIONAL LAW	GUNTHER & SULLIVAN	21.00
1081	CONSTITUTIONAL LAW	LOCKHART, K., C., S. & F.	21.00
1085	CONSTITUTIONAL LAW	ROTUNDA	23.00
1089	CONSTITUTIONAL LAW (FIRST AMENDMENT)	SHIFFRIN & CHOPER	18.00
1087	CONSTITUTIONAL LAW	STONE, S., S. & T.	22.00
1103	CONTRACTS	BARNETT	24.00
1102	CONTRACTS	BURTON	23.00
1017	CONTRACTS	CALAMARI, PERILLO & BENDER	26.00
1101	CONTRACTS	CRANDALL & WHALEY	23.00
1014	CONTRACTS	DAWSON, HARVEY & H.	22.00
1010	CONTRACTS	FARNSWORTH & YOUNG	20.00
1011	CONTRACTS	FULLER & EISENBERG	24.00
1013	CONTRACTS	KESSLER, GILMORE & KRONMAN	26.00
1016	CONTRACTS	KNAPP & CRYSTAL	23.50
1012	CONTRACTS	MURPHY & SPEIDEL	25.00
1015	CONTRACTS	ROSETT	24.00
1019	CONTRACTS	VERNON	23.00
1502	COPYRIGHT	GOLDSTEIN	21.00
1504	COPYRIGHT	JOYCE, PETRY, L. & J.	20.00
1501	COPYRIGHT	NIMMER, M., M. & N.	22.50
1218	CORPORATE TAXATION	LIND, S. L. & R	17.00
1050	CORPORATIONS	CARY & EISENBERG	22.00
1054	CORPORATIONS	CHOPER, COFFEE, & GILSON	24.50
1350	CORPORATIONS (ENTERPRISE ORG.)	CONARD, KNAUSS & SIEGEL	24.00
1053	CORPORATIONS	HAMILTON	22.00
1058	CORPORATIONS (BUSINESS ASSOCIATIONS	KLEIN, RAMSEYER & BAINBRIDGE	22.00
1057	CORPORATIONS	O'KELLEY & THOMPSON	21.00
1059	CORPORATIONS (BUSINESS ORG.)	SODERQUIST, S., C. & S.	24.00
1056	CORPORATIONS	SOLOMON, S., B. & W.	22.00
1052	CORPORATIONS	VAGTS	21.00
1300	CREDITOR'S RIGHTS (DEBTOR-CREDITOR)	RIESENFELD	24.00
1550	CRIMINAL JUSTICE	WEINREB	21.00
1029	CRIMINAL LAW	BONNIE, C., J. & L.	20.00
1020	CRIMINAL LAW	BOYCE & PERKINS	25.00
1028	CRIMINAL LAW	DRESSLER	24.00
1027	CRIMINAL LAW	JOHNSON	22.00
1021	CRIMINAL LAW	KADISH & SCHULHOFER	22.00
1026	CRIMINAL LAW	KAPLAN, WEISBERG & BINDER	21.00
1205	CRIMINAL PROCEDURE	ALLEN, KUHNS & STUNTZ	20.00
1206	CRIMINAL PROCEDURE	DRESSLER & THOMAS	25.00
1202	CRIMINAL PROCEDURE	HADDAD, Z., S. & B.	23.00
1200	CRIMINAL PROCEDURE	KAMISAR, LAFAVE & ISRAEL	22.00
1204	CRIMINAL PROCEDURE	SALTZBURG & CAPRA	20.00
1300	DEBTOR-CREDITOR (CREDITORS RIGHTS)	RIESENFELD	24.00
1304	DEBTOR-CREDITOR	WARREN & WESTBROOK	24.00
1224	DECEDENTS ESTATES (TRUSTS)	RITCHIE, A. & E.(DOBRIS/STERK).	24.00
1222	DECEDENTS ESTATES	SCOLES, HALBACH, L. & R.	24.50
	DOMESTIC RELATIONS (see FAMILY LAW)		
3000	EDUCATION LAW (COURSE OUTLINE)	AQUILA & PETZKE	28.50
1670	EMPLOYMENT DISCRIMINATION	FRIEDMAN & STRICKLER	20.00
1671	EMPLOYMENT DISCRIMINATION	ZIMMER, SULLIVAN, R. & C.	21.00
1660	EMPLOYMENT LAW	ROTHSTEIN, KNAPP & LIEBMAN	22.50
1342	ENVIRONMENTAL LAW	ANDERSON, MANDELKER & T.	19.00
1341	ENVIRONMENTAL LAW	FINDLEY & FARBER	21.00
1345	ENVIRONMENTAL LAW	MENELL & STEWART	20.00
1344	ENVIRONMENTAL LAW	PERCIVAL, MILLER, S. & L.	21.00
1343	ENVIRONMENTAL LAW	PLATER, A., G. & G.	20.00
1217	ESTATE & GIFT TAXATION	BITTKER, CLARK & McCOUCH	18.00

Ref. No.	Course	Adaptable to Courses Utilizing	Retail Price
	ETHICS (see PROFESSIONAL RESPONSIBILITY)		
1063	EVIDENCE	LEMPERT, GROSS & LIEBMAN	TBA
1066	EVIDENCE	MUELLER & KIRKPATRICK	20.00
1064	EVIDENCE	STRONG, BROUN & M.	25.50
1062	EVIDENCE	WELLBORN	25.00
1061	EVIDENCE	WALTZ & PARK	21.00
1060	EVIDENCE	WEINSTEIN, M., A. & B.	25.50
1244	FAMILY LAW (DOMESTIC RELATIONS)	AREEN	25.00
1242	FAMILY LAW (DOMESTIC RELATIONS)	CLARK & ESTIN	22.00
1245	FAMILY LAW (DOMESTIC RELATIONS)	ELLMAN, KURTZ & BARTLETT	23.00
1246	FAMILY LAW (DOMESTIC RELATIONS)	HARRIS, T. & W.	22.00
1243	FAMILY LAW (DOMESTIC RELATIONS)	KRAUSE, O., E. & G.	27.00
1240	FAMILY LAW (DOMESTIC RELATIONS)	WADLINGTON & O'BRIEN	23.00
1247	FAMILY LAW (DOMESTIC RELATIONS)	WEISBERG & APPLETON	22.00
1360	FEDERAL COURTS	FALLON, M. & S. (HART & W.)	22.00
1360	FEDERAL COURTS	HART & WECHSLER (FALLON)	22.00
1363	FEDERAL COURTS	LOW & JEFFRIES	19.00
1361	FEDERAL COURTS	McCORMICK, C. & W.	23.00
1364	FEDERAL COURTS	REDISH & SHERRY	20.00
1690	FEDERAL INDIAN LAW	GETCHES, W. & W.	23.00
1089	FIRST AMENDMENT (CONSTITUTIONAL LAW)	SHIFFRIN & CHOPER	18.00
1700	GENDER AND LAW (SEX DISCRIMINATION)	BARTLETT & HARRIS	22.00
1510	GRATUITOUS TRANSFERS	CLARK, L., M., A., & M.	21.00
1651	HEALTH CARE LAW	CURRAN, H., B. & O.	24.00
1650	HEALTH LAW	FURROW, J., J. & S.	20.50
1640	IMMIGRATION LAW	ALEINIKOFF, MARTIN & M.	19.00
1641	IMMIGRATION LAW	LEGOMSKY	22.00
1690	INDIAN LAW	GETCHES, W. & W.	23.00
1373	INSURANCE LAW	ABRAHAM	23.00
1371	INSURANCE LAW	KEETON	24.00
1370	INSURANCE LAW	YOUNG & HOLMES	20.00
1503	INTELLECTUAL PROPERTY	MERGES, M.& J.	22.00
1394	INTERNATIONAL BUSINESS TRANSACTIONS	FOLSOM, GORDON & SPANOGLE	18.00
1393	INTERNATIONAL LAW	CARTER & TRIMBLE	19.00
1392	INTERNATIONAL LAW	HENKIN, P., S. & S.	20.00
1390	INTERNATIONAL LAW	OLIVER, F., B., S. & W.	25.00
1331	LABOR LAW	COX, BOK, GORMAN & FINKIN	22.00
1471	LAND FINANCE (REAL ESTATE TRANS.)	BERGER & JOHNSTONE	21.00
1620	LAND FINANCE (REAL ESTATE TRANS.)	NELSON & WHITMAN	21.00
1452	LAND USE	CALLIES, FREILICH & ROBERTS	20.00
1421	LEGISLATION	ESKRIDGE, FRICKEY & GARRETT	18.00
1480	MASS MEDIA	FRANKLIN & ANDERSON	18.00
1312	NEGOTIABLE INSTRUMENTS (COMM. LAW)	JORDAN, WARREN & WALT	22.00
1541	OIL & GAS	KUNTZ, L., A., S. & P.	21.00
1540	OIL & GAS	MAXWELL, WILLIAMS, M. & K.	21.00
1561	PATENT LAW	ADELMAN, R., T. & W.	25.00
1560	PATENT LAW	FRANCIS & COLLINS	26.00
1310	PAYMENT LAW [SYST.][COMM. LAW]	SPEIDEL, SUMMERS & WHITE	25.00
1313	PAYMENT LAW (COMM.LAW / NEG. INST.)	WHALEY	23.00
1431	PRODUCTS LIABILITY	OWEN, MONTGOMERY & K.	25.00
1091	PROF. RESPONSIBILITY (ETHICS)	GILLERS	16.00
1093	PROF. RESPONSIBILITY (ETHICS)	HAZARD, KONIAK, & CRAMTON	21.00
1092	PROF. RESPONSIBILITY (ETHICS)	MORGAN & ROTUNDA	16.00
1094	PROF. RESPONSIBILITY (ETHICS)	SCHWARTZ, W. & P.	16.00
1030	PROPERTY	CASNER & LEACH -(by F., K. & V.	24.00
1031	PROPERTY	CRIBBET, J., F. & S.	24.50
1037	PROPERTY	DONAHUE, KAUPER & MARTIN	21.00
1035	PROPERTY	DUKEMINIER & KRIER	20.00
1034	PROPERTY	HAAR & LIEBMAN	23.50
1036	PROPERTY	KURTZ & HOVENKAMP	21.00
1033	PROPERTY	NELSON, STOEBUCK, & W.	23.50
1032	PROPERTY	RABIN & KWALL	23.00
1038	PROPERTY	SINGER	21.50
1621	REAL ESTATE TRANSACTIONS	GOLDSTEIN & KORNGOLD	21.00
1471	REAL ESTATE TRANS. & FIN. (LAND FINANCE)	BERGER & JOHNSTONE	21.00
1620	REAL ESTATE TRANSFER & FINANCE	NELSON & WHITMAN	21.00
1254	REMEDIES (EQUITY)	LAYCOCK	23.00
1253	REMEDIES (EQUITY)	LEAVELL, L., N. & K-F.	26.00
1252	REMEDIES (EQUITY)	RE & RE	26.00
1255	REMEDIES (EQUITY)	SHOBEN & TABB	25.50
1250	REMEDIES (EQUITY)	RENDLEMAN	28.00
1310	SALES (COMM. LAW)	SPEIDEL, SUMMERS & WHITE	25.00
1313	SALES (COMM. LAW)	WHALEY	23.00
1312	SECURED TRANS. (COMMERCIAL LAW)	JORDAN, WARREN & WALT	22.00
1310	SECURED TRANS.	SPEIDEL, SUMMERS & WHITE	25.00
1313	SECURED TRANS. (COMMERCIAL LAW)	WHALEY	23.00
1272	SECURITIES REGULATION	COX, HILLMAN, LANGEVOORT	21.00
1270	SECURITIES REGULATION	JENNINGS, M., C. & S.	21.00
1680	SPORTS LAW	WEILER & ROBERTS	20.50
1217	TAXATION (ESTATE & GIFT)	BITTKER, CLARK & McCOUCH	18.00
1219	TAXATION (INDIV. INCOME)	BURKE & FRIEL	22.00
1212	TAXATION (FEDERAL INCOME)	FREELAND, L., S. & L.	21.00
1211	TAXATION (FEDERAL INCOME)	GRAETZ & SCHENK	20.00
1210	TAXATION (FEDERAL INCOME)	KLEIN, BANKMAN & SHAVIRO	21.00
1218	TAXATION (CORPORATE)	LIND, S., L. & R.	17.00
1006	TORTS	DOBBS	22.00
1003	TORTS	EPSTEIN	23.50
1004	TORTS	FRANKLIN & RABIN	20.50
1001	TORTS	HENDERSON, P. & S.	23.50
1000	TORTS	PROSSER, W., S., K. & P.	25.00
1005	TORTS	SHULMAN, JAMES & GRAY	25.00
1281	TRADE REGULATION (ANTITRUST)	HANDLER, P., G. & W.	20.50
1410	U.C.C.	EPSTEIN, MARTIN, H. & N.	18.00
1510	WILLS/TRUSTS (GRATUITOUS TRANSFER)	CLARK, L., M., A., & M.	21.00
1223	WILLS, TRUSTS & ESTATES	DUKEMINIER & JOHANSON	22.00
1220	WILLS	MECHEM & ATKINSON	23.00

CASENOTES PUBLISHING CO. INC. ● 1640 FIFTH STREET, SUITE 208 ● SANTA MONICA, CA 90401 ● (310) 395-6500

E-Mail Address - info@casenotes.com
Website - www: http://www.casenotes.com

ABBREVIATIONS FOR BRIEFING

The following list of abbreviations will assist you in the process of briefing and provide an illustration of the technique of formulating functional personal abbreviations for commonly encountered words, phrases, and concepts.

acceptance	acp	offer	O
affirmed	aff	offeree	OE
answer	ans	offeror	OR
assumption of risk	a/r	ordinance	ord
attorney	atty	pain and suffering	p/s
beyond a reasonable doubt	b/r/d	parol evidence	p/e
bona fide purchaser	BFP	plaintiff	P
breach of contract	br/k	prima facie	p/f
cause of action	c/a	probable cause	p/c
common law	c/l	proximate cause	px/c
Constitution	Con	real property	r/p
constitutional	con	reasonable doubt	r/d
contract	K	reasonable man	r/m
contributory negligence	c/n	rebuttable presumption	rb/p
cross	x	remanded	rem
cross-complaint	x/c	res ipsa loquitur	RIL
cross-examination	x/ex	respondent superior	r/s
cruel and unusual punishment	c/u/p	Restatement	RS
defendant	D	reversed	rev
dismissed	dis	Rule Against Perpetuities	RAP
double jeopardy	d/j	search and seizure	s/s
due process	d/p	search warrant	s/w
equal protection	e/p	self-defense	s/d
equity	eq	specific performance	s/p
evidence	ev	statute of limitations	S/L
exclude	exc	statute of frauds	S/F
exclusionary rule	exc/r	statute	S
felony	f/m	summary judgment	s/j
freedom of speech	f/s	tenancy in common	t/c
good faith	g/f	tenancy at will	t/w
habeas corpus	h/c	tenant	t
hearsay	hr	third party	TP
husband	H	third party beneficiary	TPB
in loco parentis	ILP	transferred intent	TI
injunction	inj	unconscionable	uncon
inter vivos	I/v	unconstitutional	unconst
joint tenancy	j/t	undue influence	u/e
judgment	judgt	Uniform Commercial Code	UCC
jurisdiction	jur	unilateral	uni
last clear chance	LCC	vendee	VE
long-arm statute	LAS	vendor	VR
majority view	maj	versus	v
meeting of minds	MOM	void for vagueness	VFV
minority view	min	weight of the evidence	w/e
Miranda warnings	Mir/w	weight of authority	w/a
Miranda rule	Mir/r	wife	W
negligence	neg	with	w/
notice	mtc	within	w/I
nuisance	nus	without prejudice	w/o/p
obligation	ob	without	w/o
obscene	obs	wrongful death	wr/d

GLOSSARY

COMMON LATIN WORDS AND PHRASES ENCOUNTERED IN LAW

A FORTIORI: Because one fact exists or has been proven, therefore a second fact that is related to the first fact must also exist.

A PRIORI: From the cause to the effect. A term of logic used to denote that when one generally accepted truth is shown to be a cause, another particular effect must necessarily follow.

AB INITIO: From the beginning; a condition which has existed throughout, as in a marriage which was void ab initio.

ACTUS REUS: The wrongful act; in criminal law, such action sufficient to trigger criminal liability.

AD VALOREM: According to value; an ad valorem tax is imposed upon an item located within the taxing jurisdiction calculated by the value of such item.

AMICUS CURIAE: Friend of the court. Its most common usage takes the form of an amicus curiae brief, filed by a person who is not a party to an action but is nonetheless allowed to offer an argument supporting his legal interests.

ARGUENDO: In arguing. A statement, possibly hypothetical, made for the purpose of argument, is one made arguendo.

BILL QUIA TIMET: A bill to quiet title (establish ownership) to real property.

BONA FIDE: True, honest, or genuine. May refer to a person's legal position based on good faith or lacking notice of fraud (such as a bona fide purchaser for value) or to the authenticity of a particular document (such as a bona fide last will and testament).

CAUSA MORTIS: With approaching death in mind. A gift causa mortis is a gift given by a party who feels certain that death is imminent.

CAVEAT EMPTOR: Let the buyer beware. This maxim is reflected in the rule of law that a buyer purchases at his own risk because it is his responsibility to examine, judge, test, and otherwise inspect what he is buying.

CERTIORARI: A writ of review. Petitions for review of a case by the United States Supreme Court are most often done by means of a writ of certiorari.

CONTRA: On the other hand. Opposite. Contrary to.

CORAM NOBIS: Before us; writs of error directed to the court that originally rendered the judgment.

CORAM VOBIS: Before you; writs of error directed by an appellate court to a lower court to correct a factual error.

CORPUS DELICTI: The body of the crime; the requisite elements of a crime amounting to objective proof that a crime has been committed.

CUM TESTAMENTO ANNEXO, ADMINISTRATOR (ADMINISTRATOR C.T.A.): With will annexed; an administrator c.t.a. settles an estate pursuant to a will in which he is not appointed.

DE BONIS NON, ADMINISTRATOR (ADMINISTRATOR D.B.N.): Of goods not administered; an administrator d.b.n. settles a partially settled estate.

DE FACTO: In fact; in reality; actually. Existing in fact but not officially approved or engendered.

DE JURE: By right; lawful. Describes a condition that is legitimate "as a matter of law," in contrast to the term "de facto," which connotes something existing in fact but not legally sanctioned or authorized. For example, de facto segregation refers to segregation brought about by housing patterns, etc., whereas de jure segregation refers to segregation created by law.

DE MINIMUS: Of minimal importance; insignificant; a trifle; not worth bothering about.

DE NOVO: Anew; a second time; afresh. A trial de novo is a new trial held at the appellate level as if the case originated there and the trial at a lower level had not taken place.

DICTA: Generally used as an abbreviated form of obiter dicta, a term describing those portions of a judicial opinion incidental or not necessary to resolution of the specific question before the court. Such nonessential statements and remarks are not considered to be binding precedent.

DUCES TECUM: Refers to a particular type of writ or subpoena requesting a party or organization to produce certain documents in their possession.

EN BANC: Full bench. Where a court sits with all justices present rather than the usual quorum.

EX PARTE: For one side or one party only. An ex parte proceeding is one undertaken for the benefit of only one party, without notice to, or an appearance by, an adverse party.

EX POST FACTO: After the fact. An ex post facto law is a law that retroactively changes the consequences of a prior act.

EX REL.: Abbreviated form of the term ex relatione, meaning, upon relation or information. When the state brings an action in which it has no interest against an individual at the instigation of one who has a private interest in the matter.

FORUM NON CONVENIENS: Inconvenient forum. Although a court may have jurisdiction over the case, the action should be tried in a more conveniently located court, one to which parties and witnesses may more easily travel, for example.

GUARDIAN AD LITEM: A guardian of an infant as to litigation, appointed to represent the infant and pursue his/her rights.

HABEAS CORPUS: You have the body. The modern writ of habeas corpus is a writ directing that a person (body) being detained (such as a prisoner) be brought before the court so that the legality of his detention can be judicially ascertained.

IN CAMERA: In private, in chambers. When a hearing is held before a judge in his chambers or when all spectators are excluded from the courtroom.

IN FORMA PAUPERIS: In the manner of a pauper. A party who proceeds in forma pauperis because of his poverty is one who is allowed to bring suit without liability for costs.

INFRA: Below, under. A word referring the reader to a later part of a book. (The opposite of supra.)

IN LOCO PARENTIS: In the place of a parent.

IN PARI DELICTO: Equally wrong; a court of equity will not grant requested relief to an applicant who is in pari delicto, or as much at fault in the transactions giving rise to the controversy as is the opponent of the applicant.

IN PARI MATERIA: On like subject matter or upon the same matter. Statutes relating to the same person or things are said to be in pari materia. It is a general rule of statutory construction that such statutes should be construed together, i.e., looked at as if they together constituted one law.

IN PERSONAM: Against the person. Jurisdiction over the person of an individual.

IN RE: In the matter of. Used to designate a proceeding involving an estate or other property.

IN REM: A term that signifies an action against the res, or thing. An action in rem is basically one that is taken directly against property, as distinguished from an action in personam, i.e., against the person.

INTER ALIA: Among other things. Used to show that the whole of a statement, pleading, list, statute, etc., has not been set forth in its entirety.

INTER PARTES: Between the parties. May refer to contracts, conveyances or other transactions having legal significance.

INTER VIVOS: Between the living. An inter vivos gift is a gift made by a living grantor, as distinguished from bequests contained in a will, which pass upon the death of the testator.

IPSO FACTO: By the mere fact itself.

JUS: Law or the entire body of law.

LEX LOCI: The law of the place; the notion that the rights of parties to a legal proceeding are governed by the law of the place where those rights arose.

MALUM IN SE: Evil or wrong in and of itself; inherently wrong. This term describes an act that is wrong by its very nature, as opposed to one which would not be wrong but for the fact that there is a specific legal prohibition against it (malum prohibitum).

MALUM PROHIBITUM: Wrong because prohibited, but not inherently evil. Used to describe something that is wrong because it is expressly forbidden by law but that is not in and of itself evil, e.g., speeding.

MANDAMUS: We command. A writ directing an official to take a certain action.

MENS REA: A guilty mind; a criminal intent. A term used to signify the mental state that accompanies a crime or other prohibited act. Some crimes require only a general mens rea (general intent to do the prohibited act), but others, like assault with intent to murder, require the existence of a specific mens rea.

MODUS OPERANDI: Method of operating; generally refers to the manner or style of a criminal in committing crimes, admissible in appropriate cases as evidence of the identity of a defendant.

NEXUS: A connection to.

NISI PRIUS: A court of first impression. A nisi prius court is one where issues of fact are tried before a judge or jury.

N.O.V. (NON OBSTANTE VEREDICTO): Notwithstanding the verdict. A judgment n.o.v. is a judgment given in favor of one party despite the fact that a verdict was returned in favor of the other party, the justification being that the verdict either had no reasonable support in fact or was contrary to law.

NUNC PRO TUNC: Now for then. This phrase refers to actions that may be taken and will then have full retroactive effect.

PENDENTE LITE: Pending the suit; pending litigation underway.

PER CAPITA: By head; beneficiaries of an estate, if they take in equal shares, take per capita.

PER CURIAM: By the court; signifies an opinion ostensibly written "by the whole court" and with no identified author.

PER SE: By itself, in itself; inherently.

PER STIRPES: By representation. Used primarily in the law of wills to describe the method of distribution where a person, generally because of death, is unable to take that which is left to him by the will of another, and therefore his heirs divide such property between them rather than take under the will individually.

PRIMA FACIE: On its face, at first sight. A prima facie case is one that is sufficient on its face, meaning that the evidence supporting it is adequate to establish the case until contradicted or overcome by other evidence.

PRO TANTO: For so much; as far as it goes. Often used in eminent domain cases when a property owner receives partial payment for his land without prejudice to his right to bring suit for the full amount he claims his land to be worth.

QUANTUM MERUIT: As much as he deserves. Refers to recovery based on the doctrine of unjust enrichment in those cases in which a party has rendered valuable services or furnished materials that were accepted and enjoyed by another under circumstances that would reasonably notify the recipient that the rendering party expected to be paid. In essence, the law implies a contract to pay the reasonable value of the services or materials furnished.

QUASI: Almost like; as if; nearly. This term is essentially used to signify that one subject or thing is almost analogous to another but that material differences between them do exist. For example, a quasi-criminal proceeding is one that is not strictly criminal but shares enough of the same characteristics to require some of the same safeguards (e.g., procedural due process must be followed in a parol hearing).

QUID PRO QUO: Something for something. In contract law, the consideration, something of value, passed between the parties to render the contract binding.

RES GESTAE: Things done; in evidence law, this principle justifies the admission of a statement that would otherwise be hearsay when it is made so closely to the event in question as to be said to be a part of it, or with such spontaneity as not to have the possibility of falsehood.

RES IPSA LOQUITUR: The thing speaks for itself. This doctrine gives rise to a rebuttable presumption of negligence when the instrumentality causing the injury was within the exclusive control of the defendant, and the injury was one that does not normally occur unless a person has been negligent.

RES JUDICATA: A matter adjudged. Doctrine which provides that once a court of competent jurisdiction has rendered a final judgment or decree on the merits, that judgment or decree is conclusive upon the parties to the case and prevents them from engaging in any other litigation on the points and issues determined therein.

RESPONDEAT SUPERIOR: Let the master reply. This doctrine holds the master liable for the wrongful acts of his servant (or the principal for his agent) in those cases in which the servant (or agent) was acting within the scope of his authority at the time of the injury.

STARE DECISIS: To stand by or adhere to that which has been decided. The common law doctrine of stare decisis attempts to give security and certainty to the law by following the policy that once a principle of law as applicable to a certain set of facts has been set forth in a decision, it forms a precedent which will subsequently be followed, even though a different decision might be made were it the first time the question had arisen. Of course, stare decisis is not an inviolable principle and is departed from in instances where there is good cause (e.g., considerations of public policy led the Supreme Court to disregard prior decisions sanctioning segregation).

SUPRA: Above. A word referring a reader to an earlier part of a book.

ULTRA VIRES: Beyond the power. This phrase is most commonly used to refer to actions taken by a corporation that are beyond the power or legal authority of the corporation.

ADDENDUM OF FRENCH DERIVATIVES

IN PAIS: Not pursuant to legal proceedings.

CHATTEL: Tangible personal property.

CY PRES: Doctrine permitting courts to apply trust funds to purposes not expressed in the trust but necessary to carry out the settlor's intent.

PER AUTRE VIE: For another's life; in property law, an estate may be granted that will terminate upon the death of someone other than the grantee.

PROFIT A PRENDRE: A license to remove minerals or other produce from land.

VOIR DIRE: Process of questioning jurors as to their predispositions about the case or parties to a proceeding in order to identify those jurors displaying bias or prejudice.

NOTES

TABLE OF CASES

A

Alhakim v. Commissioner 36
Amend v. Commissioner 32
American Automobile Assoc. v. United States 43
Arkansas Best Corp. v. Commissioner 98
Armantrout v. Commissioner 85
Arrowsmith v. Commissioner 107

B

Basye, United States v. 92
Benaglia v. Commissioner 4
Biedenharn Realty Co., Inc. v. United States 96
Blackman v. Commissioner 46
Blair v. Commissioner 86
Bob Jones University v. United States 50
Brooke v. United States 90
Brown, Commissioner v. 102
Burnet v. Logan 31
Burnet v. Sanford and Brooks Co. 14

C

Carroll v. Commissioner 67
Charley v. Commissioner 5
Clark v. Commissioner 13
Corn Products Refining Co. v. Commissioner 97
Cottage Savings Assoc. v. Commissioner 29
Cramer v. Commissioner 38
Crane v. Commissioner 20

D

Danville Plywood Corporation v. United States 61
Davis, United States v. 39
Diedrich v. Commissioner 19
Diez-Arguelles v. Commissioner 41
Drescher, United States v. 34
Duberstein, Commissioner v. 8
Dyer v. Commissioner 46

E

Eisner v. Macomber 26
Encyclopedia Britannica v. Commissioner 71
Estate of Franklin v. Commissioner 79

F

Farid-Es-Sultaneh v. Commissioner 40
Ferrer, Commissioner v. 104
Flowers, Commissioner v. 63
Foglesong v. Commissioner 91

G

Georgia School Book Depository v.
     Commissioner 42
Gilbert v. Commissioner 22

Gilliam v. Commissioner 76
Gilmore, United States v. 66
Glenshaw Glass Co., Commissioner v. 7
Gregory v. Helvering 105

H

Hantzis v. Commissioner 64
Harris, United States v. 9
Heim v. Fitzpatrick 89
Helvering v. Bruun 27
Helvering v. Eubank 88
Helvering v. Hammel 108
Helvering v. Horst 87
Henderson v. Commissioner 58
Hort v. Commissioner 99

I

Inaja Land Co. v. Commissioner 12

J

Jordan Marsh Co. v. Commissioner 30

K

Kirby Lumber Co., United States v. 17
Knetsch v. United States 78

L

Lewis, United States v. 16
Lucas v. Earl 83

M

McAllister v. Commissioner 100
Merchants National Bank v. Commissioner 105
Midland Empire Packing Co. v. Commissioner 72
Miller v. Commissioner 103
Minor v. United States 35
Moller v. United States 56
Moss v. Commissioner 60

N

Nickerson v. Commissioner 55
North American Oil Consolidated v. Burnet 15
Norwest Corp. And Subsidiaries v. Commissioner .. 73

O

Ochs v. Commissioner 48
Olmsted Incorporated Life Agency v.
     Commissioner 37
Ottawa Silica Co. v. United States 49

P

P.G. Lake, Inc., Commissioner v. 101

Continued on next page.

NOTES

TABLE OF CASES (Continued)

Pevsner v. Commissioner 65
Poe v. Seaborn 84
Prosman v. Commissioner 80
Pulsifer v. Commissioner 33

R
Rudolph v. United States 59

S
Smith v. Commissioner 62
Starr's Estate v. Commissioner 74
Stephens v. Commissioner 77

T
Taft v. Bowers 11
Taylor v. Commissioner 47
Tufts, Commissioner v. 21
Turner v. Commissioner 6

V
Van Suetendael v. Commissioner 95

W
Welch v. Helvering 75
Whitten v. Commissioner 57
Williams v. McGowan 106
Woodsam Associates, Inc. v. Commissioner 28

Z
Zarin v. Commissioner 18

CHAPTER 2*
SOME CHARACTERISTICS OF INCOME

QUICK REFERENCE RULES OF LAW

1. **Noncash Benefits: Meal and Lodging Provided to Employees.** Where the economic benefits received by the employee are of a real benefit to the employer, the employee will not be taxed for them. (Benaglia v. Commissioner)

   [For more information on employee fringe benefits, see Casenote Law Outline on Federal Income Taxation, Chapter 3, § V, Exclusions from Gross Income.]

2. **Other Fringe Benefit Statutes.** Travel credits accumulated and retained by an employee in the course of his employment constitute gross income subject to taxation. (Charley v. Commissioner)

   [For more information on gross income, see Casenote Law Outline on Federal Income Taxation, Chapter 1, § III, Gross Income.]

3. **Another Approach to Valuation.** Noncash lottery-type winnings are taxable benefits even if it is difficult to assess their true value. (Turner v. Commissioner)

   [For more information on valuation, see Casenote Law Outline on Book, Chapter 1, § I.]

4. **Windfalls and Gifts: Punitive Damages.** The general definition of gross income includes all amounts recovered as the result of a lawsuit that represent an increase in wealth to the recipient and not merely compensation for noncontractual losses. (Commissioner v. Glenshaw Glass Co.)

   [For more information on punitive damages in income, see Casenote Law Outline on Federal Income Taxation, Chapter 3, § II, No Source Requirement.]

5. **Gift: The Basic Concept.** In order to be a gift under § 102, amounts received must have been given with a "detached and disinterested generosity." (Commissioner v. Duberstein)

   [For more information on gratuitous transfers, see Casenote Law Outline on Federal Income Taxation, Chapter 3, § V, Exclusions from Gross Income.]

6. **Gift: The Basic Concept.** Any person required to make a tax return who willfully fails to make such return shall, in addition to other penalties provided by law, be guilty of a misdemeanor. (United States v. Harris)

   [For more information on gifts and bequests, see Casenote Law Outline on Federal Income Taxation, Chapter 3, § V, Exclusions from Gross Income.]

7. **Transfer of Unrealized Gain by Gift While the Donor Is Alive.** The donee of a gift also accepts the donor's cost base for a determination of the tax consequences of a sale of the gift property by the donee. (Taft v. Bowers)

   [For more information on income from gifts, see Casenote Law Outline on Federal Income Taxation, Chapter 3, § V, Exclusions from Gross Income.]

8. **Recovery of Capital: Sale of Easements.** Where property is acquired in a lump sum and is subsequently disposed of a portion at a time, the sale price must be proportionally allocated to taxpayer's basis in the portion

---

*There are no cases in Chapter 1.

sold, except where apportionment would be wholly impractical or impossible. (Inaja Land Co. v. Commissioner)

[For more information on nontaxable distributions, see Casenote Law Outline on Federal Income Taxation, Chapter 4, § I, Basis.]

9. **Recovery of Loss.** Compensation paid to a taxpayer for the erroneous advice of his tax counsel which resulted in greater tax liability is not taxable as income. (Clark v. Commissioner)

10. **Annual Accounting and Its Consequences: The Use of Hindsight.** Money earned is properly taxed to the period in which it is received, even if it is attributable to work performed in a previous taxable year. (Burnet v. Sanford & Brooks Co.)

[For more information on gross income, see Casenote Law Outline on Federal Income Taxation, Chapter 1, § III, Gross Income.]

11. **Annual Accounting and its Consequences: Claim of Right.** No income has been earned where a company might never receive it and has no right to demand payment. (North American Oil Consolidated v. Burnet)

[For more information on transactional accounting, see Casenote Law Outline on Federal Income Taxation, Chapter 8, § I, The Taxable Year.]

12. **Annual Accounting and its Consequences: Claim of Right.** If a taxpayer received earnings under a claim of right and without restrictions as to its disposition, he has received income subject to tax even if his right to the money is later successfully disputed and he is forced to restore its equivalent. (United States v. Lewis)

[For more information on the "claim of right" doctrine, see Casenote Law Outline on Federal Income Taxation, Chapter 8, § I, The Taxable Year.]

13. **Transactions Involving Loans and Income from Discharge of Indebtedness: True Discharge of Indebtedness.** The retirement of debt by a corporation for less than face value represents a realized increase in net worth to the corporation and is, therefore, a taxable gain. (United States v. Kirby Lumber Co.)

[For more information on canceled debts, see Casenote Law Outline on Federal Income Taxation, Chapter 3, § III, Realized Increase in Net Wealth (or Net Worth).]

14. **Misconceived Discharge Theory.** A gambler who settles an unenforceable gambling debt does not realize income in the amount of the debt discharged by the settlement, minus the settlement amount. (Zarin v. Commissioner)

[For more information on canceled debts, see Casenote Law Outline on Federal Income Taxation, Chapter 3, § III, Realized Increase In Net Wealth (or Net Worth).]

15. **Misconceived Discharge Theory.** A donor of property whose gift tax obligation is paid by the donee realizes taxable income to the extent the gift tax paid exceeds his adjusted basis in the property. (Diedrich v. Commissioner)

[For more information on relief from debt obligations, see Casenote Law Outline on Federal Income Taxation, Chapter 4, § II, Amount Realized.]

16. **Transfer of Property Subject to Debt.** A taxpayer who sells property encumbered by a nonrecourse mortgage must include the unpaid balance of the mortgage in the computation of the amount the taxpayer realizes on the sale. (Crane v. Commissioner)

   [For more information on acquisition indebtedness, and the "Crane doctrine," see Casenote Law Outline on Federal Income Taxation, Chapter 4, § I, Basis.]

17. **Transfer of Property Subject to Debt.** The assumption of a non-recourse mortgage constitutes a taxable gain to the mortgagor even if the mortgage exceeds the fair market value of the property. (Commissioner v. Tufts)

   [For more information on nonrecourse debts, see Casenote Law Outline on Federal Income Taxation, Chapter 4, § II, Amount Realized.]

18. **Illegal Income.** A taxpayer who withdraws funds from a corporation intending to repay them and who assigns assets sufficient to cover the withdrawal does not realize income on the withdrawals. (Gilbert v. Commissioner)

   [For more information on tax on illegal gains, see Casenote Law Outline on Federal Income Taxation, Chapter 3, § II, No Source Requirement.]

BENAGLIA v. COMMISSIONER
Hotel manager (P) v. IRS (D)
36 B.T.A. 838 (1937).

NATURE OF CASE: Appeal from Commissioner's (D) assessment of deficiency tax for free rooms and meals.

FACT SUMMARY: Benaglia was the manager of a resort hotel and was required to sleep and eat there.

CONCISE RULE OF LAW: Where the economic benefits received by the employee are of a real benefit to the employer, the employee will not be taxed for them.

FACTS: Benaglia (P) was the manager of a resort hotel. He was required to be available at a moment's notice to handle any emergencies. Implicit in Benaglia's (P) contract and relationship with the hotel's owners was that he sleep and eat there. The Commissioner assessed a deficiency tax for the value of the room and meals claiming that this was compensation within the meaning of § 61(a). Benaglia (P) appealed.

ISSUE: Should an employee be taxed for fringe benefits which are granted for the convenience of the employer?

HOLDING AND DECISION: (Sternhagen, J.) No. The advantages received by the employee are mere incidents of the performance of his duty. Where the benefits are imposed upon him for the benefit of the employer, the employee should not be taxed. Benaglia (P) successfully established that his residing at the hotel and taking his meals there was an implicit part of his contractual obligation. Since this was for the convenience of his employer, it should not be taxed. The decision of the Commissioner (D) is overruled. The fact that Benaglia (P) has received some economic benefits is merely an incident of his employment and is immaterial for tax purposes.

DISSENT: (Smith, J.) The majority ignores two aspects of this case. First, it appears from correspondence between the parties that room and board was a part of the compensation for the job. Second, even if it were found that this was not the case, Benaglia (P) has received a real economic benefit. Benaglia (P) stated that it would cost him $3,600 to reside and eat elsewhere. Benaglia (P) should at least be taxed to this extent.

EDITOR'S ANALYSIS: Under § 119, the convenience doctrine is limited to meals and lodging on the employer's premises. The employee must also establish that he is "on call" outside of normal working hours. Partners and sole proprietors do not fall within the meaning of "employee." Finally, under Boykin v. Commissioner, 260 F.2d 249 (8th Cir. 1958), an employee who paid his employer rent for lodgings on the premises could exclude the value of the lodgings from his income if he could fit within the exemption provisions of § 119.

[For more information on employee fringe benefits, see Casenote Law Outline on Federal Income Taxation, Chapter 3, § V, Exclusions from Gross Income.]

QUICKNOTES

FRINGE BENEFIT - A benefit conferred on an employee by an employer in addition to the employee's salary or compensation.

NOTES:

CHARLEY v. COMMISSIONER

Frequent flyer (P) v. Commissioner (D)

91 F.3d 72 (9th Cir. 1996).

NATURE OF CASE: Appeal from tax court determination of a deficiency.

FACT SUMMARY: The Charleys (P) challenged the tax court's determination that travel credits accumulated by Philip Charley (P) in the course of his employment with Truesdail Laboratories constituted gross income subject to taxation.

CONCISE RULE OF LAW: Travel credits accumulated and retained by an employee in the course of his employment constitute gross income subject to taxation.

FACTS: Philip Charley (P) was President of Truesdail Laboratories, in which he and his wife, Katherine (P), owned 50.255% of the stock. Charley (P), in his capacity as employee, traveled to various accident sites in order to inspect allegedly defective machinery. Truesdail permitted its employees to retain any frequent flyer miles they accumulated in traveling on behalf of the company. Truesdail would bill the clients for first-class airfare, then Charley (P) would instruct the travel agent, Archer, to reserve a coach seat for himself. Charley (P) then utilized his personal frequent flyer miles in order to upgrade to first class, and directed Archer to transfer the credit balance into his personal account. In 1988, Charley (P) accumulated $3,149.93 of credit in his account. The tax court held this constituted taxable income to Charley (P), and charged him with a deficiency of $926.

ISSUE: Do travel credits accumulated and retained by an employee in the course of his employment constitute gross income subject to taxation?

HOLDING AND DECISION: (O'Scannlain, J.) Yes. Travel credits accumulated and retained by an employee in the course of his employment constitute gross income subject to taxation. Gross income is defined in Internal Revenue Code § 61 as all income from whatever source derived. In the present case, the travel credits constitute taxable income under two separate theories. First, the travel credits constitute additional compensation to Charley (P) by Truesdail. Truesdail paid for the first-class ticket, and permitted Charley (P) to utilize his frequent flyer miles and retain the difference between the first class and coach airfares. Second, assuming Charley (P) utilized his personal frequent flyer miles for the upgrade, the gain derived from the transaction constituted taxable income as a result of Charley's (P) dealing in property. The appropriate income subject to taxation in this case is the difference between the amount gained from the transaction and the property's adjusted basis. The adjusted basis of the frequent flyer miles was zero, and the total gain from the transaction was $3,149.93. Thus, under either theory the transaction resulted in taxable income to the Charleys (P) in the amount of $3,149.93. Affirmed.

EDITOR'S ANALYSIS: Note that the Tax Code does not provide a general definition of income. Gross income is defined as including all income obtained by the taxpayer in the form of cash or property. Gross income also includes all realized receipts of assets. In order for the asset to be realized, it must be sufficiently definite and identifiable.

[For more information on gross income, see Casenote Law Outline on Federal Income Taxation, Chapter 1, § III, Gross Income.]

QUICKNOTES

DEFICIENCY JUDGMENT - A judgment against a mortgagor for the difference between the amount obtained at a foreclosure sale and the amount of the mortgage debt that is due.

GROSS INCOME - The total income earned by an individual or business.

REALIZED ASSET - The incurring of a change in value as the result of an event with respect to an asset or activity, which is substantial enough to affect a person's tax liability by materially changing their economic circumstances.

NOTES:

TURNER v. COMMISSIONER
Taxpayer (D) v. IRS (P)
13 T.C.M. 462 (1954).

NATURE OF CASE: Appeal from finding of tax deficiency.

FACT SUMMARY: Turner (D) won two first-class cruise tickets from a radio show and disputed their income value with the IRS (P).

CONCISE RULE OF LAW: Noncash lottery-type winnings are taxable benefits even if it is difficult to assess their true value.

FACTS: A radio show called Turner (D) and asked him to identify a song being played. When he answered correctly, Turner (D) won two first class round-trip cruise tickets from New York to Brazil. The tickets were not transferable and good for only a year. Turner (D) negotiated with the steamship company and exchanged his winning tickets for four tickets in tourist class so that his entire family could go to Brazil. Turner (D) reported $520 as income from the winnings, but the IRS (P) determined that there was a deficiency because the retail value of the two first class tickets was $2,220. Turner (D) appealed.

ISSUE: Are noncash lottery-type winnings taxable benefits even if it is difficult to assess their true value?

HOLDING AND DECISION: Yes. Noncash lottery-type winnings are taxable benefits even if it is difficult to assess their true value. Winnings do not typically provide the beneficiaries with something they would ordinarily buy in the ordinary course of their lives. Thus, their value is not equal to their retail cost. Also, as in the present case, noncash winnings are often nontransferable and non-salable. However, these winnings do have some value when they are exchanged for some product or service. In the present case, it is virtually impossible to arrive at a proper and fair figure for the value that the winnings represented to Turner (D). The court determines that $1,400 is the fair amount of income that should have been declared by Turner (D).

EDITOR'S ANALYSIS: The decision provides no guidance whatsoever in how other courts should analyze the value of noncash winnings. The $1,400 figure just happens to be an approximation of the midway point between what Turner (D) declared and what the IRS (P) decided. The court may have decided simply to split the difference.

COMMISSIONER v. GLENSHAW GLASS CO.
IRS (D) v. Lawsuit victors (P)
348 U.S. 426 (1955).

NATURE OF CASE: Appeal from determination of tax deficiency.

FACT SUMMARY: Glenshaw Glass Co. (P) recovered compensatory and punitive damages as a result of a fraud and antitrust suit. It did not report the punitive damages as income and the IRS assessed a deficiency.

CONCISE RULE OF LAW: The general definition of gross income includes all amounts recovered as the result of a lawsuit that represent an increase in wealth to the recipient and not merely compensation for noncontractual losses.

FACTS: Two cases representing identical issues of law were consolidated for review. Glenshaw Glass Co. (P) sued a supplier for fraud and antitrust violations seeking compensatory damages and exemplary damages for the fraud and treble damages for the antitrust violations. A settlement was reached whereby Glenshaw (P) received $800,000 of which $325,000 represented punitive damages. William Goldman Theatres Inc. (P) sued another corporation for antitrust violations and was awarded $375,000 representing treble damages of the sustained loss of $125,000. Glenshaw (P) did not report the $325,000 of punitive damages as income and Goldman (P) did not report the $250,000 punitive damages. The IRS (D) assessed tax deficiencies in both instances contending the punitive damages constituted loss income as defined by § 22(a).

ISSUE: Does the general definition of gross income include all amounts recovered as the result of a lawsuit that represent an increase in wealth to the recipient rather than compensation for noncontractual losses?

HOLDING AND DECISION: (Warren, C.J.) Yes. Section 22(a), the general definition of gross income, concludes by including "gains or profits and income derived from any source whatever." This broad language has consistently been given broad application by this court. Both companies concede that the amounts recovered that represent lost profits are taxable as income. But the amounts recovered as punitive damages clearly represent an increase in wealth. If contract damage awards are taxable, it would make no sense to exclude from taxation those amounts recovered which do not represent compensation for losses but are accessions to wealth. As such they are subject to tax.

EDITOR'S ANALYSIS: Personal injury lawsuit recoveries are not subject to tax on the theory that they are roughly analogous to a return of capital and do not represent an increase in wealth to the recipient, but rather a compensation or restoration of a loss.

Contractual damage recoveries are taxable since they represent reimbursement for amounts that would have been taxable had they been received as provided for by the contract.

[For more information on punitive damages in income, see Casenote Law Outline on Federal Income Taxation, Chapter 3, § II, No Source Requirement.]

QUICKNOTES
GROSS INCOME - The total income earned by an individual or business.

PUNITIVE DAMAGES - Damages exceeding the actual injury suffered for the purposes of punishment, deterrence and comfort to plaintiff.

NOTES:

COMMISSIONER v. DUBERSTEIN
IRS (D) v. Taxpayer (P)
363 U.S. 278 (1960).

NATURE OF CASE: Actions to determine deficiencies in payment of income taxes.

FACT SUMMARY: Taxpayer-Duberstein (P) received a Cadillac in return for providing a business associate with some favorable business leads. Taxpayer-Stanton (P) received $20,000 upon his retirement from a church corporation.

CONCISE RULE OF LAW: In order to be a gift under § 102, amounts received must have been given with a "detached and disinterested generosity."

FACTS: Duberstein (P), through his company, had conducted business dealings with Berman, the president of another corporation. Duberstein (P) provided Berman with some business leads which proved so beneficial that Berman offered Duberstein a Cadillac. Although Duberstein (P) already had two cars and stated he did not intend to be compensated for the information, Berman insisted he accept the car. Berman's company later deducted the value of the car as a business expense. Stanton (P) had for 10 years been the comptroller of a church corporation, and was receiving $22,500 salary when he resigned from his position. Upon his resignation, the corporation's board of directors passed a resolution granting Stanton (P) $20,000 "in appreciation of the services rendered by" Stanton (P) for the company. There was conflicting evidence as to whether Stanton (P) received the money because of his services and because he was well-liked, or because he was forced to retire after having intervened on behalf of a discharged employee of the church.

ISSUE: In order to be a gift under § 102, must amounts received have been given with a "detached and disinterested generosity"?

HOLDING AND DECISION: (Brennan, J.) Yes. In order to be a gift under § 102, amounts received must have been given with a "detached and disinterested generosity." The car received by Duberstein (P) was deemed taxable income, but the court reversed the decision in Stanton because the factual findings did not show the legal standards used by the courts below. In reaching its decision, the court first rejected the Government's (D) proposed definition of a gift (all transfers of property made for personal and not business reasons), on the grounds that such a definition was too concise and not suitable for all the factual situations which may arise. The court then relied on previous decisions to formulate its own definition. As such, a gift is not shown by the mere absence of a legal or moral duty to make a payment, or from a lack of economic incentive, where the payments are made as compensation for services, it is irrelevant whether the donor receives any economic benefit from making the payments. As a general rule, a gift will be found where it "proceeds from a detached and disinterested generosity, out of affection, respect, admiration, charity, or like impulses," and it is the donor's intention which is controlling as to those factors. In determining the donor's intention, one must look at the facts surrounding the transfer of property, as was stated in Bogardus v. Commissioner, 302 U.S. 34. The Court then stated that since the determination of whether a payment is a gift is so closely connected to the facts of each case, an appellate court must be limited in its review of those facts. Based on these principles, the trier of fact was justified in finding that Duberstein (P) had received the car not as a gift, but as compensation for services. As to Stanton, five Justices agreed that the conclusion reached by the Tax Court could not be supported by the record, and remanded for further factual determinations.

CONCURRENCE: (Whittaker, J.) Concurrence only as to the result of Bogardus v. Commissioner required a conclusion that the determination of a "gift" is a mixed question of law and fact.

DISSENT: (Douglas, J.) In each of these cases there was a gift.

DISSENT: (Frankfurter, J.) The Court should have adopted the government's test, and held that there was presumption against a beneficiary who receives payments related to services performed.

EDITOR'S ANALYSIS: Following the Duberstein decision, lower federal courts have been reluctant to review factual determinations which are not "clearly erroneous." In restricting the power of appellate courts to review factual determinations, the Court does not fashion a test that would allow a trier of fact any guidelines to follow, and which could be a basis of review. By rejecting the government's test that gifts should be limited to personal, non-business, transactions, the Court leaves open the possibility that some gifts might be made even if part of an employer-employee relationship. However, any gifts which are made by a business, can only be deducted up to $25, as provided in § 274(b). Thus, should a business seek to deduct more than that, it must show that the payment was made for valid business reasons, and is thus deductible under § 162. Of course a showing that the dominant motive for payment was business would necessarily tend to negate a showing of a gift by the recipient of such payment.

[For more information on gratuitous transfers, see Casenote Law Outline on Federal Income Taxation, Chapter 3, § V, Exclusions from Gross Income.]

QUICKNOTES

GIFT - A transfer of property to another person that is voluntary and which lacks consideration.

UNITED STATES v. HARRIS
Federal government (P) v. Twin sister heirs (D)
942 F.2d 1125 (7th Cir. 1991).

NATURE OF CASE: Appeal from conviction for willful income tax evasion.

FACT SUMMARY: When Kritzik died after giving twin sisters, Harris (D) and Conley (D), more than half a million dollars each over the course of several years, the Government (P) alleged that the sisters had to pay income tax on the money but had willfully failed to do so.

CONCISE RULE OF LAW: Any person required to make a tax return who willfully fails to make such return shall, in addition to other penalties provided by law, be guilty of a misdemeanor.

FACTS: David Kritzik, a wealthy widower now deceased, befriended twin sisters, Lynnette Harris (D) and Leigh Ann Conley (D). Over the course of several years, Kritzik directly or indirectly gave each young woman more than half a million dollars. Either Kritzik was obligated to pay gift tax on this money or the women had to pay income tax. The Government (P) alleged that, beyond reasonable doubt, the obligation was Harris' (D) and Conley's (D). Harris (D) and Conley (D) contended that the money they received was a nontaxable gift. In separate criminal trials, Harris (D) was convicted of two counts of willfully failing to file federal income tax returns and two counts of willful tax evasion. The district court excluded as hearsay letters in which Kritzik wrote that he loved Harris (D) and enjoyed giving her things. Conley (D) was convicted of four counts of willfully failing to file federal income tax returns.

ISSUE: Shall any person required to make a tax return who willfully fails to make such return be guilty of a misdemeanor, in addition to other penalties provided by law?

HOLDING AND DECISION: Yes. Any person required to make a tax return who willfully fails to make such return shall, in addition to other penalties provided by law, shall be guilty of a misdemeanor. Each woman was required to make a return only if the money that she received from Kritzik was income to her rather than a gift. Assuming that the money was income, she acted willfully and was subject to criminal prosecution only if she knew of her duty to pay taxes and voluntarily and intentionally violated that duty. In distinguishing between income and gifts, the critical consideration is the transferor's intention. The only direct evidence the Government (P) presented in relation to Conley (D) was Kritzik's gift tax returns which substantially understated the amount of money given to her. The question is unresolved as to whether Kritzik's other payments were taxable income to Conley (D) or whether he just underreported his gifts. Conley (D) could not have "willfully" failed to pay her taxes unless she knew of

Kritzik's intent. Absent proof of Kritzik's intent and Conley's (D) knowledge of that intent, the Government (P) has no case. Furthermore, the letters from Kritzik to Harris (D), which the district court excluded as hearsay, were not hearsay because they were offered to prove Harris' (D) lack of willfulness, not for the truth of the matter asserted. The conclusion that Harris (D) should have been allowed to present the letters at issue as evidence would ordinarily lead to a remand of her case for retrial. However, current law on the tax treatment of payments to mistresses provided Harris (D) with no fair warning that her conduct was criminal. Indeed, current authorities favor Harris' (D) position that the money she received from Kritzik was a gift. Criminal prosecutions must rest on a violation of a clear rule of law. If that standard cannot be ascertained, criminal proceedings may not be used to define and punish an alleged failure to conform to those standards. Treasury regulations and federal cases are silent when it comes to the tax treatment of money transferred in the course of long-term, personal relationships. The most pertinent authority lies in several civil cases from the Tax Court which favor Harris' (D) position. If these cases make a rule of law, it is that a person is entitled to treat cash and property received from a lover as gifts, as long as the relationship consists of something more than specific payments for specific sessions of sex. When, as here, a series of cases favors the taxpayer's position, she has not been put on notice that she is in danger of crossing the line into criminality by adhering to that position. Criminal prosecutions are no place for the Government (P) to try out pioneering interpretations of tax law. Convictions reversed and remanded with instructions to dismiss the indictments.

CONCURRENCE: (Flaum, J.) The court correctly reversed both convictions. However, the path the majority takes to reach this result is troubling. Harris' (D) conviction should be found infirm because of the relative scantiness of the record. Instead, the majority distills from our gift/income jurisprudence a rule that would tax only the most base type of cash-for-sex exchange and categorically exempt from tax liability all other transfers of money and property to so-called mistresses or companions.

EDITOR'S ANALYSIS: The rule of the instant case is stated in 26 U.S.C. § 7203. Both the majority and the concurring opinions examine the U.S. Supreme Court case Commissioner v. Duberstein, 363 U.S. 278 (1960), for the proposition that the donor's intent is the "critical consideration" in distinguishing between gifts and income. In a footnote, the Seventh Circuit

Continued on next page.

declared that an injustice had been done because Harris (D) and Conley (D) had already served most of the sentences under the convictions that were reversed here. Harris (D) was sentenced to ten months in prison, and Conley (D) was sentenced to five months. The court explained that although their counsel performed well, they failed in their petitions for release pending appeal to draw the court's attention to the unique nature of their convictions under the prevailing tax cases.

_____

[For more information on gifts and bequests, see Casenote Law Outline on Federal Income Taxation, Chapter 3, § V, Exclusions from Gross Income.]

NOTES:

TAFT v. BOWERS
Stock owner (P) v. IRS (D)
278 U.S. 470 (1929).

NATURE OF CASE: Suit for refund of income taxes paid.

FACT SUMMARY: Taft (P) received a block of stock as a gift from her father. Between the time of his purchase and the time she ultimately sold the stock, the shares had appreciated in value. The IRS (D) assessed a tax on the entire appreciation while Taft (P) contended that only the appreciation from the time of her acquisition was taxable.

CONCISE RULE OF LAW: The donee of a gift also accepts the donor's cost base for a determination of the tax consequences of a sale of the gift property by the donee.

FACTS: Two companion cases presenting the same issue of law were decided by the Court. The issue presented was illustrated by example, as follows: A donor acquires 100 shares of stock for $1,000 which he retains for some period. He then makes a gift of the shares to a donee at which time their value is $2,000. The donee later sells the shares for $4,000. The position of the IRS (P) was that the entire profit over original acquisition cost (i.e., $3,000) is taxable to the donee. Taft's (P) position was that only the amount of appreciation occurring from the time of her acquisition (i.e., $2,000) is taxable to her.

ISSUE: Does the donee of a gift also accept the donor's cost base for a determination of the tax consequences of a sale of the gift by the donee?

HOLDING AND DECISION: (McReynolds, J.) Yes. It is clear that Congress intended to tax the entire profit from the time of the donor's acquisition to the time of the donee's sale of the property. The question remains as to whether Congress had the power to levy such a tax. Where an investor sells an investment at a profit, only that portion of the sale price that represents an increase over purchase price is subject to tax. The balance is considered return of capital and not taxable. Taft (P) contends that the value of the shares at the time of the gift to her represents a capital asset at that value and, therefore, only the profit over that amount is taxable. But this would permit a clear evasion of tax or a portion of the true profit. The donee, in fact, makes no capital investment in acquiring the gift. Therefore, only that portion of the sale price that represents the actual investment of capital is excludable from tax. There is nothing in the Constitution that limits the application of tax to only that appreciation that occurs while the property is in the hands of the seller. The tax levied by the IRS was correctly determined.

EDITOR'S ANALYSIS: The original purchase is excludable since this is thought to represent a gift of capital to the recipient and gifts are not taxable as income to the recipient. The cost value of the gift is now adjustable upward to reflect the amount of gift taxes paid by the donor. No income tax liability is imposed on the donor at the time of the gift since he has realized nothing by the transaction. In the case of acquisition by inheritance, the legatee takes the property with a cost basis determined at the time of the decedent donor's death.

[For more information on income from gifts, see Casenote Law Outline on Federal Income Taxation, Chapter 3, § V, Exclusions from Gross Income.]

QUICKNOTES

APPRECIATION - The increase in the fair market value of property over either an earlier value or the taxpayer's basis.

GIFT - A transfer of property to another person that is voluntary and which lacks consideration.

NOTES:

INAJA LAND CO. v. COMMISSIONER
Property owner (P) v. IRS (D)
9 T.C. 727 (1947).

NATURE OF CASE: Appeal from Commissioner's (D) assessment of tax on $50,000 settlement due to damage to taxpayer's land.

FACT SUMMARY: Inaja Land Co. (P) received $50,000 to release all claims against a city for polluting its fishing lake.

CONCISE RULE OF LAW: Where property is acquired in a lump sum and is subsequently disposed of a portion at a time, the sale price must be proportionally allocated to taxpayer's basis in the portion sold, except where apportionment would be wholly impractical or impossible.

FACTS: Inaja Land Co. (P) owned a fishing lake. It was polluted due to the construction of a tunnel. In settlement of all claims, $50,000 was awarded to Inaja (P). The Commissioner (D) claimed that a portion of this award was income and taxed Inaja Land Co. (P). Inaja (P) appealed, claiming that it was a return of capital and was not taxable. Further, Inaja (P) claimed that apportionment was not possible since the easements granted under the terms of the settlement agreement could not be measured in metes and bounds.

ISSUE: Where the extent of an injury to real property cannot be determined, should a recovery of the damage be taxable if less than the taxpayer's basis in the land?

HOLDING AND DECISION: (Leech, J.) No. A taxpayer should not be charged with gain based on pure conjecture unsupported by a foundation of ascertainable facts. Where the extent of the injury to land cannot be determined, there is no basis upon which tax liability can be assessed. The capital recovery was less than Inaja's (P) basis in the land, and so must be considered a return of capital. This is based on the rule that where property is acquired in a lump sum, the subsequent transfer of portions of it must be considered a return of capital. This is based on the rule that where property is acquired in a lump sum, the subsequent transfer of portions of it must be apportioned between the sale price of the portion and its proportionate value to the taxpayer's original basis. Where apportionment is not possible or is wholly impractical, no valuation can be made and no tax liability exists. This, of course, only applies where the sale price is less than the taxpayer's basis in the entire property. The decision of the Commissioner (D) is overruled.

EDITOR'S ANALYSIS: If the property were subsequently sold by Inaja Land (P), its basis in the property would be reduced by $50,000. Whenever capital is returned on an investment it reduces the taxpayer's basis in the property. Capital may be returned until the taxpayer's basis in the property is zero.

[For more information on nontaxable distributions, see Casenote Law Outline on Federal Income Taxation, Chapter 4, § I, Basis.]

QUICKNOTES

BASIS - The value assigned to a taxpayer's costs incurred as the result of acquiring an asset and used to compute tax amounts towards the transactions in which that asset is involved.

EASEMENT - The right to utilize a portion of another's real property for a specific use.

NOTES:

CLARK v. COMMISSIONER
Taxpayer (P) v. IRS (D)
40 B.T.A. 333, acq. 1957-1 C.B. 4 (1939).

NATURE OF CASE: Action to redetermine a deficiency assessment.

FACT SUMMARY: Clark (P) contended that a payment made by his tax attorney in compensation for a loss suffered due to the erroneous preparation of his tax return was not taxable income.

CONCISE RULE OF LAW: Compensation paid to a taxpayer for the erroneous advice of his tax counsel which resulted in greater tax liability is not taxable as income.

FACTS: Clark (P) retained a tax attorney to prepare his tax return. The attorney prepared a joint return for Clark (P) and his wife which was then filed. Subsequently, the IRS (D) audited the return and made an additional assessment against Clark (P), which he then paid. The deficiency was caused by an error on the part of the tax attorney, and Clark (P) would not have had to pay it had his attorney paid Clark (P) the amount of the deficiency as compensation for the error. The IRS (D) then assessed another deficiency, contending this payment constituted payment of Clark's (P) tax obligation by a third person, and, therefore, was taxable. Clark (P) sued for a redetermination, contending the payment was compensation for a loss, and not taxable income.

ISSUE: Is compensation paid to a taxpayer for his increased tax obligation caused by the erroneous advice of counsel taxable as income?

HOLDING AND DECISION: (Leech, J.) No. Compensation paid to a taxpayer for the erroneous advice of his tax counsel which resulted in greater tax liability is not taxable as income. The payment in this case was not for taxes. Rather, it was in compensation for erroneous tax advice which led to increased tax liability to which Clark (P) would not have been exposed without the advice. As a result, the payment was compensation for loss, which impaired Clark's (P) capital, rather than gain derived from his capital. It, therefore, was not taxable as income. Judgment for Clark (P).

EDITOR'S ANALYSIS: In this case, the court refuses to extend the doctrine enunciated in Old Colony Trust Co. v. Commissioner, 279 U.S. 716 (1929). In this case, a corporation paid its president's income tax obligation as an additional form of compensation. The Supreme Court held that such payment was taxable as income. The rationale was that the corporation's actions were tantamount to paying the officer the amount of the tax directly, and he in turn paying the tax. In this case, a different situation was perceived by the court. The payment was not for tax liability. Rather, it was compensation for a loss caused by the payor. The loss just happened to be in the form of increased tax liability.

GROSS INCOME - The total income earned by an individual or business.

NOTES:

BURNET v. SANFORD AND BROOKS CO.
IRS (D) v. Dredging company (P)
282 U.S. 359 (1931).

NATURE OF CASE: Appeal from reversal of Tax Court decision sustaining Commissioner's (D) assessment of a deficiency tax for income and profits.

FACT SUMMARY: Sanford and Brooks Co. (P) was paid under performance installments for a long-term dredging contract. Sanford and Brooks (P) brought suit when the contract was abandoned.

CONCISE RULE OF LAW: Money earned is properly taxed to the period in which it is received, even if it is attributable to work performed in a previous taxable year.

FACTS: Sanford and Brooks Co. (P) engaged in a long-term dredging operation. Payments were made each year by the other contracting party. Nonetheless, expenses exceeded payments by more than $176,000. A net operating loss was shown in 1913, 1915, and 1916. In 1915, the work was abandoned, and a suit was filed by Sanford and Brooks Co. (P) in 1916 against the other contracting party. Sanford and Brooks Co. (P) recovered their losses of $176,000 and $16,000 in interest. The Commissioner (D) assessed a delinquent tax for 1920, the year in which the suit was decided of $192,000. The court of appeals held that only the interest award of $16,000 should have been included in income. The $176,000 was merely a return of expenses previously incurred in 1913, 1915, and 1916. The Commissioner (D) appealed, claiming that the recovery was income, and the previous expenditures could not be considered.

ISSUE: Must all money that is received, excluding the sale of capital assets, in a given fiscal year be included in gross income?

HOLDING AND DECISION: (Stone J.) Yes. The money received was from a contract entered into for profit. Since no capital investments were involved, any money earned from the contract must equal gross income. The fact that no real profit was made on the contract is immaterial. The funds only become income when they are received. Net losses in previous periods have nothing to do with the current period. This rationale is consistent with the meaning and purpose of the Sixteenth Amendment. It is essential that any system of taxation produces ascertainable revenue payable at a given interval. The losses sustained could only be properly taken as deductions against income in those years. Subsequent "income" must be reported in the year it was received.

EDITOR'S ANALYSIS: Section 172 of the Code provides for a net operating loss carryback or carryover. Even if applicable, it would not have aided Sanford and Brooks Co. (P), because the income received in 1922 would have been received beyond the statutory period provided for in the Code, *i.e.*, five years.

[For more information on gross income, see Casenote Law Outline on Federal Income Taxation, Chapter 1, § III, Gross Income.]

QUICKNOTES

CAPITAL ASSET - Asset, defined in § 1221, the sale or exchange of which produces Capital Gain or Loss.

GROSS INCOME - The total income earned by an individual or business.

NOTES:

NORTH AMERICAN OIL CONSOLIDATED v. BURNET

Petroleum Company (P) v. IRS (D)

286 U.S. 417 (1932).

NATURE OF CASE: Appeal from assessment of tax liability for income allegedly earned in 1917.

FACT SUMMARY: Income earned in 1916 from property in the hands of a receiver was not reported or given to North American Oil (P) until 1917.

CONCISE RULE OF LAW: No income has been earned where a company might never receive it and has no right to demand payment.

FACTS: North American Oil (P) held oil property owned by the United States. A suit was begun to oust North American, and a receiver was appointed to manage the property and retain the income until the suit was decided. In 1917, the court decided in favor of North American (P) and income earned in 1916 was turned over to it. The government appealed, and the case was finally decided in favor of North American (P) in 1922. The Commissioner determined that the income earned in 1916 should be included in North American's 1917 income and assessed a deficiency tax on this amount. The Board of Tax Appeals found that the income was taxable to the receiver in 1916, but was overturned by the court of appeals. Certiorari was granted.

ISSUE: Should funds impounded by a receiver who is in control of only a portion of a corporation's property be taxed to the corporation when it finally has an unqualified right to receive them?

HOLDING AND DECISION: (Brandeis, J.) Yes. First, the income was not taxable to the receiver in 1916 because he was only in control of a portion of North American's property. This is consistent with long-standing Treasury regulations. Next, the income could not be taxed to North American (P) in 1916, because it might never receive the funds. The first time North American (P) had an unqualified right to the funds was after the district court awarded them to it in 1917. At that time the receivership was vacated, North American (P) had a claim for the money, and actually received it. The fact that the case was not ultimately settled until 1922 is immaterial. If North American (P) had lost, it would have repaid the funds out of current assets and taken a deduction for that amount. The funds received in 1917 should have been reported as income for that year. The decision of the court of appeals is affirmed.

EDITOR'S ANALYSIS: Other examples of the above-mentioned situation occur where reserves are set up which exceed actual costs or expenditures. And, for the cash or accrual taxpayer, income must be reported when it is received, even if it will not be earned until a subsequent tax year.

[For more information on transactional accounting, see Casenote Law Outline on Federal Income Taxation, Chapter 8, § I, The Taxable Year.]

QUICKNOTES

RECEIVER - An individual who is appointed in order to maintain the holdings of a corporation, individual or other entity that is insolvent.

NOTES:

UNITED STATES v. LEWIS
Federal government (D) v. Taxpayer (P)
340 U.S. 590 (1951).

NATURE OF CASE: Suit for refund of income taxes paid.

FACT SUMMARY: Lewis (P) erroneously received a $22,000 bonus from his employer and reported it as income. He was later forced to repay $11,000 and he sought to refigure his tax return for the year of receipt. The IRS (D) contended the $11,000 returned should be taken as a loss in a later year.

CONCISE RULE OF LAW: If a taxpayer received earnings under a claim of right and without restrictions as to its disposition, he has received income subject to tax even if his right to the money is later successfully disputed and he is forced to restore its equivalent.

FACTS: In 1944, Lewis (P) received a bonus of $22,000 from his employer and he reported it as income for that year and paid the tax due thereon. Subsequently, the employer brought suit to recover $11,000 of the bonus on the basis that the amount had been paid erroneously. A judgment in favor of the employer was rendered in state court in 1946 and Lewis (P) repaid the $11,000. Between the time of original payment and the time of repayment pursuant to the judgment Lewis used the $22,000 unconditionally as his own. The trial court concluded that his receipt of the full $22,000 was in good faith but mistaken. Lewis (P) sought to refigure his 1944 tax return to reflect the receipt of only an $11,000 bonus in that year. The IRS (D) contended that he should claim the $11,000 repayment as a loss on his 1946 return.

ISSUE: If a taxpayer receives earnings under a claim of right and without restrictions as to its disposition, has he received income subject to tax even if his right to the money is later successfully disputed and he is forced to restore its equivalent?

HOLDING AND DECISION: (Black, J.) Yes. Income taxes must be paid on income earned during an annual accounting period. Where a taxpayer receives earnings under a claim of right and without restrictions on its use, he has received income subject to tax. The "claim of right" doctrine is used to give finality to the accounting period. If the taxpayer is later forced to pay all or part of the income received, he may claim it as a loss in the period of payback. This case is not analogous to that of an embezzler since he receives the embezzled money without any claim or right either equitable or legal. Lewis is not entitled to recompute his taxes for 1944, but may claim a loss in 1946.

EDITOR'S ANALYSIS: The obvious problem presented in this case arises when the tax liability in the later years is less than in the year at receipt. The tax savings realized by the taxpayer by claiming a loss may not equal the amount of tax originally paid on the disputed income. A later enacted code section (§ 1341) designed to specifically handle this type of problem gives the taxpayer several options in order that he might regain the tax paid without a recomputation at the year of receipt.

[For more information on the "claim of right" doctrine, see Casenote Law Outline on Federal Income Taxation, Chapter 8, § I, The Taxable Year.]

QUICKNOTES

BASIS - The value assigned to a taxpayer's costs incurred as the result of acquiring an asset and used to compute tax amounts towards the transactions in which that asset is involved.

CLAIM OF RIGHT - Person claiming a right in property is in possession and intends to claim ownership of that property without regard to the record title owner.

NOTES:

16

UNITED STATES v. KIRBY LUMBER CO.
Federal government (D) v. Bond issuer (P)
284 U.S. 1 (1931).

NATURE OF CASE: Suit for refund of income taxes paid.

FACT SUMMARY: Kirby Lumber (P) issued bonds at par value and then later repurchased some of them in the open market below par. The IRS (D) contended the difference between the issuing price and the repurchase price was a taxable gain to Kirby Lumber (P).

CONCISE RULE OF LAW: The retirement of debt by a corporation for less than face value represents a realized increase in net worth to the corporation and is, therefore, a taxable gain.

FACTS: Kirby Lumber (P) issued bonds having a par value of $12,127,000, for that amount. Later in the same year it was able to repurchase a part of the bonds for a price below par. The aggregate difference in price between the par value and repurchase price was $138,000. The IRS assessed a tax on that amount contending it was a taxable gain to Kirby Lumber (P). Kirby (P) paid the tax and sued for a refund.

ISSUE: Does retirement of debt for less than face value represent a taxable gain to a corporation?

HOLDING AND DECISION: (Holmes, J.) Yes. Section 16(a) defines gross income as gains or profits and income derived from any source whatever. The retirement of debt for less than face or issuing value represents a gain or income for the taxable year. By this transaction, Kirby (P) made available $138,000 previously offset by the bond obligations. This represented an accession to income within the popular meaning of those words and is a taxable event.

EDITOR'S ANALYSIS: The proceeds of a loan are not taxable to the borrower and the repayment of the principal is not deductible since neither transaction affects the borrowers net worth. An issue arises however, when the liability is discharged without repayment by the borrower. Where a father relinquishes a liability from the son, this can quite properly be considered a gift of that amount and not taxable to the son. Where the debt is repaid through services, rather than in cash, the debt reduction would clearly be income.

[For more information on cancelled debts, see Casenote Law Outline on Federal Income Taxation, Chapter 3, § III, Realized Increase in Net Wealth (or Net Worth).]

QUICKNOTES

PAR VALUE - The stated value of a security.

TAXABLE GAIN - A recognition of increase in income that may be subject to income tax.

NOTES:

ZARIN v. COMMISSIONER
Gambler (D) v. IRS (P)
916 F.2d 110 (3rd Cir. 1990).

NATURE OF CASE: Appeal from tax court assessment of tax deficiency.

FACT SUMMARY: Zarin (D) appealed from an order of the tax court assessing a tax deficiency of approximately $5.2 million against him, arguing that he did not recognize income in that amount as a result of a discharge of a gambling debt by settlement.

CONCISE RULE OF LAW: A gambler who settles an unenforceable gambling debt does not realize income in the amount of the debt discharged by the settlement, minus the settlement amount.

FACTS: Zarin (D) racked up gambling debts of $3,435,000 with Resorts International. The amount of the debt was discharged in a settlement for $500,000. The Commissioner (P) determined that Zarin (D) realized income in the amount of $2,935,000, reflecting the difference between the debt and the settlement, and determined Zarin's (D) deficiency to be $2,047,245. The tax court agreed, and with interest, the deficiency amounted to approximately $5.2 million. From that order Zarin (D) appealed, arguing that he did not realize income from release of a portion of the debt.

ISSUE: Does a gambler who settles an unenforceable gambling debt realize income in the amount of the debt discharged by the settlement, minus the settlement amount?

HOLDING AND DECISION: (Cowen, J.) No. A gambler who settles an unenforceable gambling debt does not realize income in that amount of the debt discharged by the settlement, minus the settlement amount. Gross income generally includes income from the discharge of indebtedness, but only as to any indebtedness for which the taxpayer is liable, or an indebtedness as to which the taxpayer holds property. Zarin (D) was not liable for the indebtedness, since the gambling debt he owed was unenforceable as a matter of state law. Further, he did not have a debt subject to which he held property. The chips he held were merely an accounting mechanism to evidence debt. The best approach is to view the gambling debt as a disputed debt or one of contested liability. Zarin's (D) settlement only served to fix the amount of the debt. Fixed as such, Zarin (D) realized no income from the settlement and should have realized no income from the discharge of the disputed debt. Reversed.

DISSENT: (Stapleton, J.) The tax consequences in this particular circumstance should turn on the manner in which the parties treated the debt. Zarin (D) received value (the enjoyment of gambling) and should be taxed on the amount discharged as realized income.

EDITOR'S ANALYSIS: It seems somewhat incongruous that one who gambles with money is conceptually different from one who gambles with gaming chips. If the two are equated, it would seem that the notes taken by resorts evidencing the debts could be enforced in the same manner as another note evidencing a loan. However, it would appear that the fact that gambling debts were specifically unenforceable by state law was the point on which the case actually turned. If the debt could not legally be collected, it was not a debt for tax purposes.

[For more information on cancelled debts, see Casenote Law Outline on Federal Income Taxation, Chapter 3, § III, Realized Increase In Net Wealth (or Net Worth).]

QUICKNOTES

DISCHARGE OF DEBTS - In bankruptcy, the relief of a debtor, who is unable to pay his debts as they become due, from the obligation to pay his creditors.

GROSS INCOME - The total income earned by an individual or business.

NOTES:

DIEDRICH v. COMMISSIONER
Donors of Stock (P) v. IRS (D)
457 U.S. 191 (1982).

NATURE OF CASE: Appeal of a tax deficiency action.

FACT SUMMARY: In separate actions, the IRS (D) claimed a gift tax paid by donees of stock constituted taxable income to Diedrich (P) and Grant (P), the donors.

CONCISE RULE OF LAW: A donor of property whose gift tax obligation is paid by the donee realizes taxable income to the extent the gift tax paid exceeds his adjusted basis in the property.

FACTS: In separate cases, Diedrich (P) and Grant (P) made gifts of stock to relatives conditioned upon the donees paying the gift tax. In both cases, the gift tax paid exceeded the donor's adjusted bases in the stock. On audit, the IRS (D) claimed the donors realized income to the extent the tax paid exceeded their adjusted bases in the property. The Tax Court concluded the donors had made a "net gift" of the difference between the fair market value and the gift tax paid. The court of appeals consolidated the appeals and reversed.

ISSUE: Does a donor of property whose gift tax liability is assumed by the donee realize taxable income to the extent the tax paid exceeds his adjusted basis in the property?

HOLDING AND DECISION: (Burger, J.) Yes. A donor of property whose gift tax liability on the transaction is assumed by the donees realizes taxable income to the extent the tax paid exceeds his adjusted basis in the property. One whose tax liability is assumed by another realizes an economic benefit from the relief of indebtedness. It is as if the amount of tax paid was given to the donor as payment for the property and the donor then paid the tax himself. The substance of the transaction prevails over the form. Therefore, a conditional gift as in this case is considered a part sale, with the price in the amount of the tax, and a part gift of the value of the property which exceeds the tax. Therefore, the donor realizes gain in the amount of the tax paid which exceeds his adjusted basis in the property. Affirmed.

DISSENT: (Rehnquist, J.) The basis of the majority opinion is in the cases of Old Colony Trust v. Comm., 279 U.S. 716, and Crane v. Comm., 331 U.S. 1, where the fact of a taxable event was undisputed. The majority here assumed without analysis that in fact a taxable event occurs upon a conditional gift because Congress did not establish that a partial sale occurs upon a conditional gift of this sort, no taxable event has occurred and therefore, no gain is realized.

EDITOR'S ANALYSIS: This case illustrates that the Court will look beyond the form of the transaction and recognize economic gain when the substance of the transaction points to it. The court did recognize in a footnote that "[b]y treating conditional gifts as part gift and part sale, income is realized only when highly appreciated property is transferred, for only highly appreciated property will result in a gift tax greater than the adjusted basis."

[For more information on relief from debt obligations, see Casenote Law Outline on Federal Income Taxation, Chapter 4, § II, Amount Realized.]

QUICKNOTES

ADJUSTED BASIS - The occurrence of events with respect to an asset that require a corresponding increase or decrease in the value a taxpayer assigns to the costs expended in acquiring that asset, to reflect the occurrence of those events.

GIFT TAX - A tax levied on the transfer of property that is made as a gift.

NOTES

CRANE v. COMMISSIONER

Apartment building inheritor (P) v. Commissioner (D)

331 U.S. 1 (1947).

NATURE OF CASE: Review of judgment upholding determination of deficiency.

FACT SUMMARY: Crane (P) inherited real property subject to an unassumed mortgage.

CONCISE RULE OF LAW: A taxpayer who sells property encumbered by a nonrecourse mortgage must include the unpaid balance of the mortgage in the computation of the amount the taxpayer realizes on the sale.

FACTS: Crane (P) inherited an apartment building. The building had a mortgage on it which, when combined with unpaid interest exactly equaled the estate tax appraiser's valuation of the building and property. Crane (P) did not assume the mortgage. She agreed to remit the net rental proceeds after taxes to the mortgagee. Some six years later, faced with the threat of foreclosure, Crane (P) sold the property and received $2,500 in cash for it (net). Crane (P) included $1,250 in her income for the year on the theory that the property was a capital asset; her original basis in the property was zero; and, therefore, one-half the profits had to be included as income from the sale of a capital asset. The Commissioner (D) levied a deficiency tax. He claimed that her basis was the fair market price at the time of acquisition, less allowable depreciation. Therefore, Crane (P) actually realized a net taxable gain of $2,500 in cash plus six years of depreciation deductions, a total of $23,767.03. Crane (P) argued that only her equity in the property could be considered as her basis. Since it was zero to begin with, no depreciation was allowed. Since she only realized $2,500 in cash, this was all that could be taxed. The tax court found in her favor, but the appeals court reversed. The Supreme Court granted certiorari.

ISSUE: Must a taxpayer who sells property encumbered by a nonrecourse mortgage include the unpaid balance of the mortgage in the computation of the amount the taxpayer realizes on the sale?

HOLDING AND DECISION: (Vinson, C.J.) Yes. A taxpayer who sells property encumbered by a nonrecourse mortgage must include the unpaid balance of the mortgage in the computation of the amount the taxpayer realizes on the sale. Section 113(a)(5) states that the basis for property received by inheritance is the fair market value of the property on the date of acquisition. "Value" is nowhere defined or treated as synonymous with "equity." Therefore, Crane's (P) basis in the apartment was $262,045, *i.e.*, its fair market value at date of acquisition. The apartment building was an asset subject to exhaustion through wear and tear used in Crane's (P) trade or business. Section 113(b)(1)(B) requires that proper adjustments to basis shall be made in such cases. On sale of the asset, the seller realizes any cash received plus the amount of the indebtedness on the property. This is necessary to compute the selling price which must be subtracted from the taxpayer's adjusted basis to compute a loss or gain on the transaction. Adjusted basis is defined under Section 113(b)(1)(B) as the basis less allowance for depreciation of the asset whether or not actual deductions were taken. The difference between the selling price and Crane's (P) adjusted basis is $23,767.03. Crane (P) actually took most of the deductions allowed her by law. Crane (P) used these deductions to reduce her income. Crane (P) cannot be allowed the benefit of such deductions with no corresponding gain as of the date of sale. The Commissioner was correct in determining that she realized $257,500 on the sale of the property. Affirmed.

DISSENT: (Jackson, J.) When Crane (P) acquired the property it was in default and could have been immediately foreclosed. Under such circumstance, she actually received nothing of value. When she later sold the property, there was no accompanying release of debt since she had never assumed the mortgage and was not personally liable. Her net profit on the transaction was $2,500. The depreciation issue is not before the court and it need not decide whether deductions were properly taken.

EDITOR'S ANALYSIS: In determining profit or loss on the disposition of an asset, liens and other indebtedness are not considered. The formula is fair market value at date of acquisition minus depreciation (if allowed) equals adjusted basis. This is subtracted from the selling price. It is immaterial whether the lien has gotten greater or smaller during the interim. If the selling price is greater than the adjusted basis, a profit has been made which is taxable even if, because of an increase in mortgage indebtedness, the taxpayer receives no money.

[For more information on acquisition indebtedness, and the "Crane doctrine," see Case note Law Outline on Federal Income Taxation, Chapter 4, § I, Basis.]

QUICKNOTES

ADJUSTED BASIS - The occurrence of events with respect to an asset that require a corresponding increase or decrease in the value a taxpayer assigns to the costs expended in acquiring that asset, to reflect the occurrence of those events.

DEPRECIATION - An amount given to a taxpayer as an offset to gross income, to account for the reduction in value of the taxpayer's income producing property due to everyday usage.

PROFIT - An amount gained above those monies or value paid in the form of costs.

COMMISSIONER v. TUFTS
IRS (D) v. Taxpayer (P)
461 U.S. 300 (1983).

NATURE OF CASE: Appeal from a deficiency assessment.

FACT SUMMARY: Tufts (P) contended that the assumption of mortgage which exceeded the fair market value of the property by the purchaser was not a taxable event.

CONCISE RULE OF LAW: The assumption of a nonrecourse mortgage constitutes a taxable gain to the mortgagor even if the mortgage exceeds the fair market value of the property.

FACTS: Tufts (P) and others entered into a partnership with Pelt, a builder who had previously entered into an agreement with Farm and Home Savings to transfer a note and deed of trust to the bank in return for a loan to construct an apartment complex in the amount of $1,851,500. The loan was made on a nonrecourse basis in that neither the partnership nor the partners assumed personal responsibility for repayment. A year after construction was completed, the partnership could not make the mortgage payments, and each partner sold his interest to Bayles. The fair market value of the property at the time of the transfer did not exceed $1,400,000. As consideration, Bayles paid each partner's sale expenses and assumed the mortgage. The IRS (D) assessed a deficiency against each partner, contending the assumption of the mortgage constituted the creation of taxable gain to each of them which they failed to report. Tufts (P) and the others sued for a redetermination, contending that no gain was realized because the mortgage exceeded the fair market value of the property. The Tax Court upheld the deficiencies, and the court of appeals reversed. The Supreme Court granted certiorari.

ISSUE: Does the assumption of a nonrecourse mortgage constitute a taxable gain to the mortgagor even if the mortgage exceeds the fair market value of the property?

HOLDING AND DECISION: (Blackmun, J.) Yes. The assumption of a nonrecourse mortgage constitutes a taxable gain to the mortgagor even if the mortgage exceeds the fair market value of the property. When a mortgage is executed, the amount is included, tax free, in the mortgagor's basis of property. The amount is tax free because of the mortgagor's obligation to repay. Unless the outstanding amount of an assumed mortgage is calculated in the seller's amount realized, the money originally received in the mortgage transaction will forever escape taxation. When the obligation to repay is canceled, the mortgagor is relieved of his responsibility to repay the amount he originally received. Therefore, he realizes value to the extent of the relief from debt. When the obligation is assumed, it is as if the mortgagor was paid the amount in cash and then paid the mortgage off. As such, it is clearly income and taxable. Reversed.

CONCURRENCE: (O'Connor, J.) The situation presented in this case is easily analyzed if the purchase of the property, the mortgage, and the assumption of the mortgage are treated as separate events. This clarifies the situation as merely one of debt relief and demonstrates beyond doubt that the assumption of the mortgage was a taxable event.

EDITOR'S ANALYSIS: This case illustrates that the cost basis of the property under I.R.C. § 1012 is the cost of the property including any amount paid with borrowed funds. These funds must be included regardless of their source. When property is purchased subject to debt, the purchaser is deemed to have received cash in the amount of the debt, in turn, to have used it to purchase the property.

[For more information on nonrecourse debts, see Casenote Law Outline on Federal Income Taxation, Chapter 4, § II, Amount Realized.]

QUICKNOTES
ASSUMPTION - Laying claim to or taking possession of.

BASIS - The value assigned to a taxpayer's costs incurred as the result of acquiring an asset and used to compute tax amounts towards the transactions in which that asset is involved.

NONRECOURSE - Status of person who holds an instrument which gives him no legal right against prior endorsers or the drawer to compel payment if the instrument is dishonored.

NOTES:

GILBERT v. COMMISSIONER
Stockholder (P) v. IRS (D)
552 F.2d 478 (2d Cir. 1977).

NATURE OF CASE: Appeal from judgment holding unauthorized corporate withdrawals taxable income.

FACT SUMMARY: The Tax Court held that Gilbert (P) had realized income when he made unauthorized withdrawals of funds from E.L. Bruce & Co., Inc. to pay for stock losses.

CONCISE RULE OF LAW: A taxpayer who withdraws funds from a corporation intending to repay them and who assigns assets sufficient to cover the withdrawal does not realize income on the withdrawals.

FACTS: Gilbert (P), president and principal stockholder of E.L. Bruce & Co., Inc., a lumber supply business, purchased, on margin, stock in another lumber supply business, intending to merge the two companies. He also induced the corporation to buy stock in the company. Subsequently, the stock market declined, and Clark (P) instructed the secretary of the corporations to use corporate funds to supply cash needed to meet the margin call. From the outset, Gilbert (P) intended to repay these funds and believed he was acting in the corporation's best interest. Gilbert (P) then consulted attorneys concerning the withdrawals, and on their advice, he executed interest-bearing promissory notes to the corporation, secured by an assignment of his property, the value of which exceeded the amount of the withdrawals. The IRS (D) subsequently assessed a deficiency, contending Gilbert (P) realized taxable income from the withdrawals. The Tax Court upheld the deficiencies, and Gilbert (P) appealed.

ISSUE: Does a taxpayer realize taxable income on unauthorized corporate withdrawals made with the intent to repay?

HOLDING AND DECISION: (Lombard, J.) No. A taxpayer who, without formal authorization, withdraws funds from his corporation with the intent to repay and who assigns assets to the corporation to secure notes executed pursuant to the intent to repay does not realize taxable income in the withdrawals. In this case, Gilbert (P) should not be taxed as an embezzler who receives unauthorized use of funds with which he is entrusted. Rather he is more accurately described as a borrower who realizes no taxable gain from the loan because of the concomitant obligation to repay. Gilbert's (P) actions were taken to further the interest of the corporation by affecting a favorable merger. He almost immediately executed the notes and assigned his property to ensure repayment. As a result, the withdrawals did not constitute taxable illegal income, and the deficiencies were erroneous. Reversed.

EDITOR'S ANALYSIS: Illegal income, such as that gained through larceny, robbery, or embezzlement, is fully taxable. As a result, a person who commits a relatively minor theft offense may be found guilty of federal tax evasion for failing to report the illegal gain as taxable income. Although some commentators find it distasteful for the federal government to share in ill-gotten gain, it is this theory of the taxability of illegal income that allowed the government to successfully prosecute and imprison several notorious criminals, including Al Capone. Unable to convict him of several murders and robberies he was suspected of committing, the government successfully prosecuted Capone for income tax evasion due to his failure to report illegal income.

[For more information on tax on illegal gains, see Casenote Law Outline on Federal Income Taxation, Chapter 3, § II, No Source Requirement.]

NOTES:

CHAPTER 3
PROBLEMS OF TIMING

QUICK REFERENCE RULES OF LAW

1. **Gains and Losses from Investment in Property: Origins.** Income is gain derived and severed from capital or labor or both. (Eisner v. Macomber)

   [For more information on stock dividends, see Casenote Law Outline on Federal Income Taxation, Chapter 3, § IV, Some Instances in Which Gross Income (Other Than Gain) Is Deferred Pending Some Later "Realization" Event.]

2. **Gains and Losses from Investment in Property: Development-Tenant Improvements.** Income has been realized by a lessor when he regains possession of property upon which the lessee has made valuable improvements. (Helvering v. Bruun)

   [For more information on lessee improvements, see Casenote Law Outline on Federal Income Taxation, Chapter 3, § IV, Some Instances in Which Gross Income (Other Than Gain) Is Deferred Pending Some Later "Realization" Event.]

3. **Gains and Losses from Investment in Property: Nonrecourse Borrowing in Excess of Basis.** If a taxpayer obtains a loan on which he is not personally liable by mortgaging property whose basis is less than the loan proceeds, there is no basis for including in his income those loan proceeds in excess of his basis in the property or for changing his basis in it. (Woodsam Associates, Inc. v. Commissioner)

   [For more information on deferral of gain and loss, see Casenote Law Outline on Federal Income Taxation, Chapter 4, § IV, Recognition of Gains and Losses.]

4. **Gains and Losses from Investment in Property: Losses.** A financial institution realizes tax-deductible losses when it exchanges its interests in one group of residential mortgage loans for another lender's interests in a different group of residential mortgage loans. (Cottage Savings Association v. Commissioner)

   [For more information on gains and losses, see Casenote Law Outline on Federal Income Taxation, Chapter 4, § III, Realization.

5. **Gains and Losses from Investment in Property: Express Nonrecognition Provisions.** A transaction wherein capital invested in real estate is completely liquidated for cash in an amount equal to the value of a fee estate is a sale. (Jordan Marsh Co. v. Commissioner)

   [For more information on like kind exchanges, see Casenote Law Outline on Federal Income Taxation, Chapter 4, § IV, Recognition of Gains and Losses.]

6. **Open Transactions.** Where property is sold for less than its fair value, and, as part of the compensation, the seller is to receive an additional indeterminate and speculative amount in the future, the transaction is deemed as "open" sale and no tax is assessed until the seller recovers his basis in the property. (Burnet v. Logan)

   [For more information on "open transactions," see Casenote Law Outline on Federal Income Taxation, Chapter 4, § IV, Recognition of Gains and Losses.]

7. **Constructive Receipt and Related Doctrines: Basic Principles.** A cash basis taxpayer cannot be deemed to have realized income at the time a promise to pay in the future is made, and the doctrine of constructive receipts should not be applied to such income. (Amend v. Commissioner)

[For more information on constructive receipt, see Casenote Law Outline on Federal Income Taxation, Chapter 8, § II, Tax Accounting Methods.]

8. **Constructive Receipt and Related Doctrines: Basic Principles.** Under the economic benefit theory, a cash basis taxpayer may be taxed on the economic and financial benefit derived from the absolute right to income in the form of a fund which has been irrevocably set aside in trust for him and is beyond the reach of the payor's debtors. (Pulsifer v. Commissioner)

[For more information on the economic benefit doctrine, see Casenote Law Outline on Federal Income Taxation, Chapter 8, § II, Tax Accounting Methods.]

9. **Retirement Benefits: Early Case Law.** An annuity policy purchased by an employer for an employee is income to the employee even though held by the employer and not assignable. (United States v. Drescher)

[For more information on annuities, see Casenote Law Outline on Federal Income Taxation, Chapter 5, § III, Income Security Investments.]

10. **Deferred Compensation.** Where a taxpayer participates in a deferred compensation plan which establishes a trust to which the participating taxpayer has no vested, funded right, the contributions to the plan are not currently taxable. (Minor v. United States)

[For more information on deferred compensation, see Casenote Law Outline on Federal Income Taxation, Chapter 8, § II, Tax Accounting Methods.]

11. **Deferred Compensation.** An amount transferred by an obligee equal to the obligation may be something other than income. (Al-Hakim v. Commissioner)

[For more information on loan transactions, see Casenote Law Outline on Federal Income Taxation, Chapter 3, § III, Realized Increase in Net Wealth (or Net Worth).]

12. **Deferred Compensation.** Periodic payments made in consideration of the surrender of rights to future payments are taxable only upon receipt. (Commissioner v. Olmsted Incorporated Life Agency)

[For more information on annuities, see Casenote Law Outline on Federal Income Taxation, Chapter 5, § III, Income Security Investments.]

13. **Nonstatutory Stock Options.** Stock options that do not have a readily ascertainable value at the time they are granted are not considered income at that time unless they are tranferable, immediately exercisable and not subject to restrictions. (Cramer v. Commissioner)

[For more information on stock options, see Casenote Law Outline on Book, Chapter 1, § I.]

14. **Property Settlements: Transfers Incident to a Divorce or Separation Agreement.** The transfer of property pursuant to a marital settlement agreement is a taxable event. Taxes are computed based on the fair market value of the property at the time of transfer. (United States v. Davis)

[For more information on exchanges between related parties, see Casenote Law Outline on Federal Income Taxation, Chapter 4, § IV, Recognition of Gains and Losses.]

15. **Property Settlements: Antenuptial Settlements.** In an antenuptial agreement, shares of stock received from one who lacked donative intent and given in exchange for a fair consideration are not a gift under I.R.C.

§ 1015(a). (Farid-Es-Sultaneh v. Commissioner)

[For more information on transfers between husband and wife, see Casenote Law Outline on Federal Income Taxation, Chapter 4, § I, Basis.]

16. **Child Support Obligations in Default.** Amounts due to a taxpayer for child support are not deductible under I.R.C. § 166 as a nonbusiness bad debt. (Diez-Arguelles v. Commissioner)

[For more information on debt discount, see Casenote Law Outline on Federal Income Taxation, Chapter 4, § III, Realization.]

17. **Cash Receipts and Payments of Accrual-Method Taxpayers: Delay in the Receipt of Cash.** Under the accrual basis of taxpayer accounting when the right to receive an amount becomes fixed, the right accrues rendering the amount taxable income. (Georgia School Book Depository v. Commissioner)

[For more information on the accrual method of accounting, see Casenote Law Outline on Federal Income Taxation, Chapter 8, § II, Tax Accounting Methods.]

18. **Cash Receipts and Payments of Accrual-Method Taxpayers: Prepaid Income.** The Commissioner of Internal Revenue did not abuse his discretion in determining that annual dues paid in advance by members of an accrual-basis automobile club at various times during the year may not be ratably apportioned by the club over the 12-month membership period. (American Automobile Association v. United States)

[For more information on prepaid income, see Casenote Law Outline on Federal Income Taxation, Chapter 8, § II, Tax Accounting Methods.]

EISNER v. MACOMBER
IRS (D) v. Stockholder (P)
252 U.S. 189 (1920).

NATURE OF CASE: Appeal from judgment denying imposition of a tax on a stock dividend.

FACT SUMMARY: The Government (D) attempted to impose a tax on a stock dividend received by Macomber (P), contending such dividends were taxable as income.

CONCISE RULE OF LAW: Income is gain derived and severed from capital or labor or both.

FACTS: Macomber (P) owned 2,200 shares of stock in Standard Oil Company of California, each with a par value of $100. In 1916, the company declared a 50 percent stock dividend whereby each stockholder received one new share for every two old shares. Macomber (P) received 1,100 new shares for a total of 3,300 shares. The issuance of the stock dividend had no effect whatsoever on the underlying value of the stock. Macomber's (P) stock before the dividend was $360 to $382 per share, and after the dividend the stock was worth $234 to $268 per share, yet her total wealth was not altered by the dividend because the total value of the company, and, therefore, her pro rata share of that value, remained the same. The Government (D) contended the stock dividend constituted taxable income. Macomber (P) sued to redetermine her tax liability, and the district court held the dividend was not income. The Government (D) appealed.

ISSUE: Is a stock dividend considered income for taxation purposes?

HOLDING AND DECISION: (Pitney, J.) No. Income for taxation purposes is defined as gain which is derived and severed from capital or labor or both. A stock dividend does not constitute a severance of the stockholder's interest in the corporation; it merely represents a change in the evidence which represents that interest. As every shareholder's interest is increased proportionately, no individual interest is affected. Therefore, there is no derivative gain realized on a stock dividend and no income is produced. Affirmed.

DISSENT: (Holmes, J.) The term, "income," should be given its common law meaning, and a stock dividend would, under that meaning, constitute income.

DISSENT: (Brandeis, J.) This method of stock dividend issuance is tantamount to a corporation issuing stock options on a pro rata basis to its shareholders and simultaneously issuing a cash dividend to be used to buy the stock. The pure stock dividend merely eliminates the cash disbursement and issues the stock in the first instance. Because there is no substantive difference in the methods, the stock dividend should be as subject to taxation as the option method.

EDITOR'S ANALYSIS: This case is a landmark in the law of taxation and is codified today in I.R.C. § 305(a). It has been limited by § 305 (b) in that a stock dividend may be subject to taxation if the shareholder had the option of receiving a cash or stock dividend. A stock dividend may also be taxed where it results in a change in the nature of the shareholder's investment or proportionate interest.

[For more information on stock dividends, see Casenote Law Outline on Federal Income Taxation, Chapter 3, § IV, Some Instances in Which Gross Income (Other Than Gain) Is Deferred Pending Some Later "Realization" Event.]

QUICKNOTES
PAR VALUE - The stated value of a security.

STOCK DIVIDEND - Distributing stock as a dividend. It is a proportional distribution of shares without payment of consideration to existing shareholders.

NOTES:

HELVERING v. BRUUN
IRS (D) v. Property owner (P)
309 U.S. 461 (1940).

NATURE OF CASE: Appeal by Commissioner (D) from Tax Court's determination that no gain had been realized by lessor due to lessee's improvements to the property.

FACT SUMMARY: Lessee built a new building on Bruun's (P) land.

CONCISE RULE OF LAW: Income has been realized by a lessor when he regains possession of property upon which the lessee has made valuable improvements.

FACTS: Bruun (P) leased a lot and building (as leasor) for 99 years. The lease contained a provision that the tenant, for a certain sum, could demolish the building and build a new structure. In 1929, the lessee built a new building with a useful life of no more than 50 years, which was less than the time remaining on the lease. In 1933, Bruun (P) reentered the land and took possession of it and the new building due to lessee's default. The Commissioner (D) assessed a tax on the enhanced value of the land with the new building less the undepreciated value of the old building which had been destroyed. The courts below overruled the Commissioner (D) finding that no income had been generated. This appeal was then taken.

ISSUE: Is taxable income realized when a lessor regains possession of property upon which the tenant has made improvements?

HOLDING AND DECISION: (Roberts, J.) Yes. The taxpayer contends that the asset was a capital asset when it was obtained, the improvement cannot be severed and it remains a capital asset until sold. Therefore, no taxable income is generated until it has been disposed of. Section 61(a) is broad enough to embrace the gain in question. This situation is different from stock splits where the shareholder's proportionate interest remains the same. Here, Bruun, upon repossession of the property, received a building worth approximately $50,000 more than the old one. The value of his land had been substantially improved. Realization of gain need not be in cash or result from the sale of an asset. The fact that gain is a portion of the value of property received in the transaction does not negate its realization. It is also not necessary to be able to sever the improvement. Bruun (P) realized gain on the transaction and must be taxed accordingly.

EDITOR'S ANALYSIS: Section 109 was added to the Code to eliminate the harshness of the Bruun ruling. This section provides that gross income will not include a lessee's improvements upon the termination of the lease. However, if the improvements were made in lieu of rent or as part of the inducement for granting the lease, they will be taxed to the lessor.

[For more information on lessee improvements, see Casenote Law Outline on Federal Income Taxation, Chapter 3, § IV, Some Instances in Which Gross Income (Other Than Gain) Is Deferred Pending Some Later "Realization" Event.]

QUICKNOTES

CAPITAL ASSET - Asset, defined in § 1221, the sale or exchange of which produces capital gain or loss.

REALIZATION - General principle under which gains and losses are deemed to "exist" for income tax purposes only when "realized," referring to some event which marks the taxpayer's change of status with respect to the asset, principally as the result of sale, exchange, or disposition. A "deemed realization rule" is one wherein the tax law treats a nonrealization event as a realization event.

NOTES:

WOODSAM ASSOCIATES, INC. v. COMMISSIONER
Taxpayer (P) v. IRS (D)
198 F.2d 357 (2d Cir. 1952).

NATURE OF CASE: Action challenging the computation of an adjusted basis.

FACT SUMMARY: Mrs. Wood took out a $400,000 mortgage, for which she was not personally liable, on property in which she had an adjusted basis of $270,000. Woodsam (P) then acquired it by exchange.

CONCISE RULE OF LAW: If a taxpayer obtains a loan on which he is not personally liable by mortgaging property whose basis is less than the loan proceeds, there is no basis for including in his income those loan proceeds in excess of his basis in the property or for changing his basis in it.

FACTS: By use of a "dummy," Mrs. Wood managed to avoid personal liability when she took out a $400,000 mortgage on property in which she had an adjusted basis of only $270,000. Woodsam (P) then acquired the property in a tax-free exchange, meaning it would take over whatever was Mrs. Wood's proper adjusted basis in the property. Eventually, the aforementioned mortgage was foreclosed. In computing the gain or loss it realized upon sale by foreclosure, Woodsam (P) used a basis the Commissioner (D) held was incorrect. It sought a review of that decision, claiming Mrs. Wood had received taxable income to the extent the mortgage proceeds exceeded her basis in the property. Thus, her basis in the property would be increased by that amount and Woodsam (P) would be entitled to that stepped-up basis. The tax court disagreed with Woodsam (P), finding that it simply took over a $270,000 basis.

ISSUE: Does a taxpayer receive taxable income to the extent that the proceeds from a mortgage loan for which he is not personally liable exceed his adjusted basis in the mortgage property?

HOLDING AND DECISION: (Chase, C.J.) No. A taxpayer does not receive taxable income to the extent that the proceeds from a mortgage loan for which he is not personally liable exceed his adjusted basis in the mortgaged property, so the loan effects no change in the basis he has in said property. The mortgage loan transaction did not effect a disposition of the property. If there was no disposition, there could be no taxable event and no taxation of gain. Since taxation of gain would be what allowed a taxpayer to increase his adjusted basis in the property, the absence of such taxation in this case prevented any increase in the adjusted basis of the property Mrs. Wood owned. Affirmed.

EDITOR'S ANALYSIS: The method of borrowing cited in this case serves as an example of one of the many ways property owners can utilize some of the equity built up in their property without suffering an immediate tax-penalty. They simply borrow against their appreciated property and use the resulting funds as a source for other investment ventures or even as spendable income.

[For more information on deferral of gain and loss, see Casenote Law Outline on Federal Income Taxation, Chapter 4, § IV, Recognition of Gains and Losses.]

NOTES:

COTTAGE SAVINGS ASSOC. v. COMMISSIONER
Financial institution (P) v. IRS (D)
111 S. Ct. 1503 (1991).

NATURE OF CASE: Appeal from denial of tax deduction.

FACT SUMMARY: When Cottage Savings (P) declared a tax loss on exchanges of interests in mortgage loans, the Commissioner (D) disallowed the deduction.

CONCISE RULE OF LAW: A financial institution realizes tax-deductible losses when it exchanges its interests in one group of residential mortgage loans for another lender's interests in a different group of residential mortgage loans.

FACTS: On December 31, 1980, Cottage Savings (P) sold "90% participation" in 252 mortgages to four savings and loans and simultaneously purchased "90% participation interests" in 305 mortgages held by these S&Ls. The fair market value of the participation interests exchanged by each side was approximately $4.5 million. The face value of the participation interests Cottage Savings (P) relinquished was approximately $6.9 million. Cottage Savings (P) claimed a reduction for $2,447,091 on its federal income tax return for 1980. This amount represented the adjusted difference between the face value of the participation interests that it traded and the fair market value of the participation interests that it received. After the Commissioner (D) of Internal Revenue disallowed the deduction, the Tax Court held that it was permissible. The court of appeals reversed on the ground that the losses were not "actually" sustained during the 1980 tax year for purposes of § 165(a) of the Code.

ISSUE: Does a financial institution realize tax-deductible losses when it exchanges its interests in one group of residential mortgage loans for another lender's interests in a different group of residential mortgage loans?

HOLDING AND DECISION: (Marshall, J.) Yes. A financial institution realizes tax-deductible losses when it exchanges its interests in one group of residential mortgage loans for another lender's interests in a different group of residential mortgage loans. The Internal Revenue Code defers the tax consequences of a gain or loss in property value until the taxpayer "realizes" the gain or loss. Under the Code, an exchange of property gives rise to a realization event so long as the exchanged properties are "materially different" — that is, so long as they embody legally distinct entitlements. Because the participation interests exchanged by Cottage Savings (P) and the other S&Ls derived from loans that were made to different obligors and secured by different homes, the exchanged interests did embody legally distinct entitlements. Thus, Cottage Savings (P) realized its losses at the point of the exchange. Furthermore, § 165(a) of the Code states that a deduction shall be allowed for "any loss sustained during the taxable year and not compensated for by insurance or otherwise." Only a bona fide loss is allowable. Since

there was no contention that the transactions in this case were not bona fide, Cottage Savings (P) sustained its losses within the meaning of § 165(a). Reversed and remanded.

DISSENT: (Blackmun, J.) That the partial interests exchanged were "different" was not in dispute. The materiality prong should have been the focus. A material difference is one that has the capacity to influence a decision. The application of this standard could lead to only one answer — that the mortgage participation partial interests released were not materially different from the mortgage participation partial interests received.

EDITOR'S ANALYSIS: When interest rates soared during the late 1970s and early 1980s, the fair market value of mortgages held at much lower interest rates by the nation's thrift institution declined by over a trillion dollars. By selling mortgages and buying similar mortgages, or swapping mortgages, the thrifts hoped to amass huge tax losses without substantially altering their asset portfolios. Reporting these losses consistent with the then-effective Federal Home Loan Banking Board accounting regulations would have placed many S&Ls at risk of closure. In response to this situation, the FHLBB determined that S&Ls did not have to report losses associated with mortgages that were exchanged for "substantially identical" mortgages held by other lenders. The Court declared that mortgages could be substantially identical for FHLBB purposes yet still exhibit "differences" of a "material" nature for federal tax purposes.

[For more information on gains and losses, see Casenote Law Outline on Federal Income Taxation, Chapter 4, § III, Realization.]

QUICKNOTES

REALIZATION - General principle under which gains and losses are deemed to "exist" for income tax purposes only when "realized," referring to some event which marks the taxpayer's change of status with respect to the asset, principally as the result of sale, exchange, or disposition. A "deemed realization rule" is one wherein the tax law treats a nonrealization event as a realization event.

NOTES:

JORDAN MARSH CO. v. COMMISSIONER
Property owner (P) v. IRS (D)
269 F.2d 453 (2d Cir. 1959).

NATURE OF CASE: Appeal from judgment upholding the disallowance of a deduction.

FACT SUMMARY: The IRS (D) contended that a transaction whereby Marsh (P) transferred property and then immediately leased it for 30 years was not a sale and, therefore, disallowed the deduction of basis taken by Marsh (P) on the amount realized.

CONCISE RULE OF LAW: A transaction wherein capital invested in real estate is completely liquidated for cash in an amount equal to the value of a fee estate is a sale.

FACTS: Marsh (P) conveyed two parcels of land, with a combined adjusted basis of $4.8 million upon which it operated a department store. In return, Marsh (P) received $2.3 million in cash, the fair market value of the properties, and leases on the properties for terms of 30 years and three days with options to renew for another 30 years. The conveyances were unconditional and the leases were for normal rental amounts. Treating the conveyance as a sale, Marsh (P) deducted its loss calculated by subtracting the basis from the amount realized on the transaction. The IRS (D) disallowed the deduction, contending the leases constituted a reconveyance of a fee estate in the land and, therefore, the transaction was not a sale, but a like kind exchange under I.R.C. § 1031(a), which did not permit the recognition of gain or loss. The Tax Court upheld the disallowance, and Marsh (P) appealed.

ISSUE: Is the liquidation of capital in real estate for a property's fair market value and subsequent leaseback for an extended period a sale of the property?

HOLDING AND DECISION: (Hincks, J.) Yes. A transaction wherein capital in real estate is completely liquidated for cash in an amount equal to the property's fair market value is a sale. The leaseback situation in this case came after Marsh (P) had liquidated its entire capital investment in the property. It received the full value for the fee estate it owned. It, in all senses of the term, cashed in its investment. Clearly, then, it conveyed a fee estate and received cash and then entered into a long-term lease. This constituted a sale of the property, allowing the deduction of basis from the amount realized on the sale. Reversed.

EDITOR'S ANALYSIS: This case suggests that if Marsh (P) had received a lease for less than the fair rental value of the property, or if it had received less than the $2.3 million, the transaction may have been classified as an exchange. Although there is some disagreement whether the exchange of a fee interest for a long-term lease is an exchange of property of a like kind, Regulation § 1031(a)–1(c) states that a 30-year leasehold exchanged for a fee qualifies as a like kind exchange. Similarly, longer leaseholds, such as 95 years, have qualified. Twenty-five-year leaseholds have been held not to be of a like kind as a fee interest, however.

[For more information on like kind exchanges, see Casenote Law Outline on Federal Income Taxation, Chapter 4, § IV, Recognition of Gains and Losses.]

QUICKNOTES

ADJUSTED BASIS - The occurrence of events with respect to an asset that require a corresponding increase or decrease in the value a taxpayer assigns to the costs expended in acquiring that asset, to reflect the occurrence of those events.

BASIS - The value assigned to a taxpayer's costs incurred as the result of acquiring an asset and used to compute tax amounts towards the transactions in which that asset is involved.

FAIR MARKET VALUE - The price of particular property or goods that a buyer would offer and a seller accept in the open market, following full disclosure.

NOTES:

BURNET v. LOGAN
IRS (D) v. Stockholder (P)
283 U.S. 404 (1931).

NATURE OF CASE: Appeal by Commissioner (D) from a decision of the court of appeals overruling his assessment of an income tax on an alleged "closed" sale.

FACT SUMMARY: As part of their compensation for the sale of their stock in Andrews and Hitchcock Co., the shareholders were to be paid $0.60 per ton of ore taken each year from a leased mine.

CONCISE RULE OF LAW: Where property is sold for less than its fair value, and, as part of the compensation, the seller is to receive an additional indeterminate and speculative amount in the future, the transaction is deemed as "open" sale and no tax is assessed until the seller recovers his basis in the property.

FACTS: Logan (P) owned 250 of the 4,000 shares in Andrews and Hitchcock Iron. The corporation obtained a 97-year lease on mining property. It was not required, under the lease, to mine a minimum or maximum amount of ore each year. The shareholders, including Logan (P), sold all of their shares in Andrews and Hitchcock to Youngstown Sheet and Pipe. They received less than the fair market value of their stock in cash. As additional compensation, Youngstown agreed to pay the shareholders $0.60 per ton of ore mined each year under the 97-year lease. Logan (P) also received half of the payments made to her mother's estate under her mother's will. This was valued at $277,000 for estate tax purposes. Logan (P) paid no taxes on any of the payments received from Youngstown since she had not yet recovered her basis in the stock and the payments received by her based on her mother's stock had not yet reached the assessed estate tax amount. The Commissioner (D) found that the payments to be made by Youngstown had an ascertainable value, the sale was a "closed" transaction, and all payments should be allocated between return of capital and income. The district court sustained the Commissioner (P), but was overruled by the court of appeals which held that this was an "open" transaction and Logan (P) was entitled to recover her basis before taxes could be assessed.

ISSUE: Where the amount to be received by a seller is indeterminate and speculative, can the seller recover his basis before sustaining any tax liabilities?

HOLDING AND DECISION: (McReynolds, J.) Yes. There is no way to adequately determine the value of the $0.60 per ton payments by Youngstown. It was not required to mine any minimum or maximum amount a year; the value of the ore remaining in the mine is uncertain; Youngstown's future needs could not be predicted. Therefore, there is no way to estimate the value of Logan's (P) interest in the $0.60 per ton payments. The transaction was a sale and the promise to pay $0.60 per ton cannot be considered an equivalent to cash. It has no ascertainable fair market value. Since Logan (P) received less than the fair market value of the stock when it was sold, she is entitled to recover her basis before sustaining tax liabilities. The sale was an "open" transaction. Once Logan (P) recovers her basis, subsequent payments will represent gain and will be taxed as such. As far as the payments received under her mother's will, the same rationale applies. Until they began to exceed the appraised valuation no tax liability accrues to her. Logan (P) takes her mother's basis in the property and the transaction is still considered an "open" sale. The Commissioner's decision is overruled.

EDITOR'S ANALYSIS: It is very rare that a transaction will be considered to be open. If the lease had called for the mining and sale of specific amounts of ore each year, the result may have been different. The Court might have found that the value of the contract right to receive $0.60 per ton could be determined. Courts generally tend to valuate assets, if at all possible, even though the estimate may be exceedingly "rough."

[For more information on "open transactions," see Casenote Law Outline on Federal Income Taxation, Chapter 4, § IV, Recognition of Gains and Losses.]

QUICKNOTES

FAIR MARKET VALUE - The price of particular property or goods that a buyer would offer and a seller accept in the open market, following full disclosure.

NOTES:

AMEND v. COMMISSIONER
Farmer (D) v. IRS (P)
13 T.C. 178 (1949).

NATURE OF CASE: Action in Tax Court.

FACT SUMMARY: Amend (D) sold wheat to Burris in 1944 with the understanding that the wheat would be shipped at once and that Burris would pay for it in January 1945.

CONCISE RULE OF LAW: A cash basis taxpayer cannot be deemed to have realized income at the time a promise to pay in the future is made, and the doctrine of constructive receipts should not be applied to such income.

FACTS: In 1944, Amend (D) sold 30,000 bushels of wheat to Burris at $1.57 per bushel. The understanding was that Amend (D) would ship the wheat at once, and Burris would pay for it in January 1945. The wheat was shipped in August and was paid for by a check dated January 1945. The Commissioner contends that the amount received for the wheat should be included in Amend's (D) 1944 income.

ISSUE: Can a cash basis taxpayer be deemed to have realized income at the time a promise to pay in the future is made?

HOLDING AND DECISION: (Black, J.) No. A cash basis taxpayer cannot be deemed to have realized income at the time a promise to pay in the future is made. The doctrine of constructive receipts should not be applied to such income. The basis of that doctrine is that, for taxation purposes, income is received or realized when it is made subject to the will and control of the taxpayer and can be, except for his own action or inaction, reduced to actual possession. Such was not the case here. Amend (D) had no legal right to demand and receive his money from the sale of his 1944 wheat until January 1945, under his contract with Burris. Since Amend (D) had no unqualified right to receive the money for his wheat in the year when the contract was made, and since his failure to receive his money was not of his own volition, the doctrine of constructive receipts does not apply.

EDITOR'S ANALYSIS: Ross v. Comm., 169 F.2d 483, held that a taxpayer could rely on the doctrine of constructive receipt to defeat the Commissioner's assertion of a deficiency for the year of actual payment, even though the amounts in question had not been reported by him in the earlier years, which were now barred by the statute of limitations. The amounts in question (accrued salary) had been credited to the taxpayer on the books of his employer, which was an the accrual basis, and deducted by it. The court held that the taxpayer was not estopped or otherwise barred by equitable considerations, partly because there was no misrepresentation of the facts. "A mere failure to report income is not a representation that such income has in fact not been received. Inasmuch as the tax incidence of so many transactions is as doubtful as it is, from the mere failure to report no more significant inference should be drawn than the taxpayer's own interpretation of the law."

[For more information on constructive receipt, see Casenote Law Outline on Federal Income Taxation, Chapter 8, § II, Tax Accounting Methods.]

QUICKNOTES

CASH BASIS - The value assigned to a taxpayer's costs incurred as the result of acquiring an asset and used to compute tax amounts towards the transactions in which that asset is involved.

CONSTRUCTIVE RECEIPT (OF INCOME) - Taxable income which is unqualifiedly subject to the demand of taxpayer on cash receipts and disbursements method of accounting, whether or not such income has actually been received in cash.

NOTES:

PULSIFER v. COMMISSIONER
Sweepstakes winners (P) v. IRS (D)
64 T.C. 245 (1975).

NATURE OF CASE: Appeal from a deficiency assessment.

FACT SUMMARY: The Pulsifers (P) contended that sweepstakes winnings which were withheld from them due to their minority were not an economic benefit to them until they received them, and therefore, were not income until then.

CONCISE RULE OF LAW: Under the economic benefit theory, a cash basis taxpayer may be taxed on the economic and financial benefit derived from the absolute right to income in the form of a fund which has been irrevocably set aside in trust for him and is beyond the reach of the payor's debtors.

FACTS: Gordon Pulsifer purchased an Irish Hospital Sweepstakes ticket in his name and in the names of his three minor children, Stephen (P), Susan (P), and Thomas (P), in 1969. His ticket won, yet when he attempted to claim the money, the children's share was withheld and deposited in trust with the Bank of Ireland for the children, to be released upon their reaching majority or until demand for release of the funds was made by their legal representative. The Commissioner of the IRS (D) assessed a deficiency against the children for failing to pay taxes on the winnings while they were being held in trust. The Pulsifers (P) sued in Tax Court, contending all they had in 1969 was a non-assignable chose in action, and the winnings were, therefore, not income under the economic benefit theory asserted by the Commissioner.

ISSUE: Under the economic benefit theory, may a cash basis taxpayer be taxed on the economic and financial benefit derived from the absolute right to income held in trust for him?

HOLDING AND DECISION: (Hall, J.) Yes. Under the economic benefit theory, a cash basis taxpayer may be taxed on the economic and financial benefit derived from the absolute right to income in the form of a fund which has been irrevocably set aside in trust for him and is beyond the reach of the payor's creditors. In this case, the children had a absolute right to the winnings and all they needed was a legal representative to claim it. As a result, they had the economic benefit of the money in 1969, when it was, therefore, taxable. Judgment for the Commissioner (D).

EDITOR'S ANALYSIS: This case illustrates the theory that income will be recognized when its economic benefit is bestowed. Some commentators argue this case could have been decided, with a similar conclusion, under the doctrine of constructive receipt. That doctrine holds that income is taxable, even though not in the taxpayer's possession, when it is credited to his account or otherwise set apart for him.

[For more information on the economic benefit doctrine, see Casenote Law Outline on Federal Income Taxation, Chapter 8, § II, Tax Accounting Methods.]

QUICKNOTES

CASH BASIS - The value assigned to a taxpayer's costs incurred as the result of acquiring an asset and used to compute tax amounts towards the transactions in which that asset is involved.

CHOSE IN ACTION - The right to recover, or the item recoverable, in a law suit.

NOTES:

UNITED STATES v. DRESCHER
IRS (P) v. Taxpayer (D)
179 F.2d 863 (2d Cir. 1950); cert. denied, 340 U.S. 821 (1950).

NATURE OF CASE: The Commissioner (D) appealed from a tax court decision that no income was received through the purchase of a single payment annuity.

FACT SUMMARY: Drescher's (P) employer purchased two single payment annuities for him which were not reported as additional compensation by Drescher (P).

CONCISE RULE OF LAW: An annuity policy purchased by an employer for an employee is income to the employee even though held by the employer and not assignable.

FACTS: Drescher's (P) employer purchased two annuity contracts for Drescher. It retained the policies and they were not assignable. Drescher (P) was to receive income from them upon retirement. No income was reported by Drescher (P) concerning the annuities. The Commissioner (D) assessed a delinquent tax holding that they were additional compensation. Drescher (P) claimed that he received nothing because no income would be received until he retired. The Tax Court found for Drescher (P) and the case was appealed.

ISSUE: Is deferred compensation in the form of an annuity includable in present income?

HOLDING AND DECISION: (Swan, J.) Yes. It cannot be doubted that Drescher (P) received some current value from the purchase of the annuities. It was compensation and represented an economic benefit to Drescher (P). The question of how to value it does not have to be reached by the court. Drescher (P) must establish the extent to which he was overtaxed. He claimed the full contract price was not includable in income and this is clearly incorrect. At a minimum, he must be taxed on the present value of the life insurance feature of the annuity. Since Drescher (P) has not met his burden of proof, the decision of the Tax Court must be overruled.

CONCURRENCE AND DISSENT: (Clark, J.) The entire amount paid for the annuity should be taxed. It relieves taxpayers such as Drescher (P) from the responsibility of providing for their own retirement.

EDITOR'S ANALYSIS: If taxpayer purchases an annuity with his own funds, then there is no tax liability until payments are received. Sections 401, 402, and 403 were added to the Code and tightened restrictions on the taxability of both qualified and nonqualified plans.

[For more information on annuities, see Casenote Law Outline on Federal Income Taxation, Chapter 5, § III, Income Security Investments.]

NOTES:

MINOR v. UNITED STATES
Physician (P) v. Federal government (D)
772 F.2d 1472 (9th Cir. 1985).

NATURE OF CASE: Appeal from award of tax refund.

FACT SUMMARY: The Government (D) appealed from a decision awarding a tax refund to Minor (P), contending that contributions made by Minor (P) to a deferred compensation plan were currently taxable to him.

CONCISE RULE OF LAW: Where a taxpayer participates in a deferred compensation plan which establishes a trust to which the participating taxpayer has no vested, funded right, the contributions to the plan are not currently taxable.

FACTS: Minor (P) is a physician who entered into an agreement with Snohomish Physicians to provide services to prepaid medical plan members in accordance with an established fee schedule. He entered into a Supplemental Agreement whereby the participating physician could utilize deferred compensation. Under the plan, Minor (P) elected the percentage of fees he was to be actually paid, with the remainder going into the deferred compensation fund. For years 1970, 1971, and 1973, he elected to receive 10 percent of the fees. Snohomish Physicians established a trust fund to provide for its financial obligations under the Supplemental Agreement. Snohomish Physicians was the settlor and the beneficiary while three physicians, including Minor (P), were trustees. Retirement annuity policies were purchased to provide for the payment of benefits under the plan, payable to the physician or his beneficiary upon death, disability, retirement or departure from the plan. The physicians agreed to provide services under the Agreement until benefits under the plan became payable, and also to limit practice after retirement, provide certain emergency and consulting services, and to refrain from participating in competing groups. During the years 1970, 1971, and 1973, Minor (P) included only the 10 percent of fees actually received as gross income. The Government (D) contended that the amount paid into the deferred compensation trust was includable in gross income. Minor (P) paid the disputed amount of tax and successfully sued for a refund. From the decision awarding Minor (P) the tax refund, the Government (D) appealed.

ISSUE: Where a taxpayer participates in a deferred compensation plan which establishes a trust to which the participating taxpayer has no vested, funded right, are the contributions to the plan currently taxable?

HOLDING AND DECISION: No. Where a taxpayer participates in a deferred compensation plan which establishes a trust to which the participating taxpayer has no vested, funded right, the contributions to the plan are not currently taxable. [The Government (D) conceded that Minor (P) did not actively or constructively receive the 90 percent of the fees paid into the deferred compensation trust.] In the present case, Minor's (P) interest in the assets of the trust is neither secured nor non-forfeitable. Snohomish Physicians is both settlor and beneficiary of the trust, and therefore, the deferred compensation plan is unfunded and confers no presently taxable economic benefit. Secondly, Minor's (P) right to receive benefits under the deferred compensation plan are subject to a number of conditions, subject to a risk of forfeiture. Since the plan is an unfunded, unsecured plan subject to a risk of forfeiture, the economic benefit doctrine is inapplicable, and the plan confers no currently taxable benefit upon Minor (P). Affirmed.

EDITOR'S ANALYSIS: Had the trust assets in the present case not been subject to the creditors of the Snohomish Physicians, as they were both settlor and beneficiary, Minor (P) may have had a secured interest in the trust assets. Some employees have avoided the constructive receipt problem through utilizing a loan arrangement, instead of receiving advance payments of deferred compensation.

[For more information on deferred compensation, see Casenote Law Outline on Federal Income Taxation, Chapter 8, § II, Tax Accounting Methods.]

QUICKNOTES

ANNUITY - The payment or right to receive payment of a fixed sum periodically, for a specified time period.

DEFERRED COMPENSATION - Earnings that are to be taxed at the time that they are received by, or distributed to, the employee and not when they are in fact earned.

NOTES:

ALHAKIM v. COMMISSIONER
Sports agent (P) v. IRS (D)
T.C.M. 136 (1987).

NATURE OF CASE: Review of deficiency assessment.

FACT SUMMARY: Al-Hakim (P) received a loan in the amount of a fee due to be paid to him.

CONCISE RULE OF LAW: An amount transferred by an obligee equal to the obligation may be something other than income.

FACTS: Al-Hakim (P) negotiated a contract for major league baseball player Lyman Bostock. His fee was to be $112,500, payable in equal installments over 10 years. Bostock then "loaned" Al-Hakim (P) this same amount, interest-free, to be repaid over 10 years. The result was that for each installment due Al-Hakim (P), an installment would be due Bostock, and the obligations would cancel each other. The IRS (D) contended that Al-Hakim (P) had in fact been fully paid his fee, and made a deficiency assessment. Al-Hakim filed a Tax Court action.

ISSUE: May an amount transferred by an obligee equal to the obligation be something other than income?

HOLDING AND DECISION: Yes. An amount transferred by an obligee equal to the obligation may be something other than income. Here, the documentation supports the contention that the $112,500 paid to Al-Hakim (P) was a loan, not a fee. Judgment for Al-Hakim (P).

EDITOR'S ANALYSIS: Loans are not considered to be taxable income. The obvious reason for this is that they are to be paid back. This gives taxpayers great motivation to try to disguise payments as loans. A good number of Tax Court decisions deal with this issue.

[For more information on loan transactions, see Casenote Law Outline on Federal Income Taxation, Chapter 3, § III, Realized Increase in Net Wealth (or Net Worth).]

COMMISSIONER v. OLMSTED INCORPORATED LIFE AGENCY

IRS (D) v. Insurance agent (P)

304 F.2d 16 (8th Cir. 1962).

NATURE OF CASE: Appeal from a Tax Court decision reversing a finding of taxable income.

FACT SUMMARY: The IRS (D) contended that Olmsted (P) realized taxable income when it received a contract whereby it would be paid in monthly payments for a period of 15 years in consideration for its surrender of all rights to future renewal commissions on previously written insurance policies.

CONCISE RULE OF LAW: Periodic payments made in consideration of the surrender of rights to future payments are taxable only upon receipt.

FACTS: Olmstead Incorporated Life Agency (Olmstead) (P) was the exclusive insurance agent in Iowa for Peoples Life Insurance Co. (Peoples). Prior to his death, Miller, Olmstead's (P) president and principal stockholder, entered into a contract wherein all of Olmsteads's (P) rights to renewal commissions earned after January 1, 1956, were assigned to Peoples in return for an annuity calling for payment of $500 per month for 15 years. In 1956, Olmstead's (P) corporate tax return declared income of $5,500, representing the annuity payments received that year. The IRS (D) assessed a deficiency, contending the entire contract value was taxable income in 1956. The Tax Court held the contract was not fully taxable in 1956, and the IRS (D) appealed.

ISSUE: Do contracts calling for present periodic payments to be made in consideration of the surrender of right to future payments constitute taxable income on the effective date of the contract?

HOLDING AND DECISION: (Vogal, J.) No. Periodic payments made in consideration of the surrender of rights to future payments are taxable only upon receipt. In this case, Olmstead (P) did not reduce the future commission payments to his immediate possession. It took no dominion over the accrued commissions other than to agree to receive them in cash installments as they accrued under the contract. Until the payments are made, Olmstead (P) derives no economic benefit from the contract. As a result, the payments are taxable upon receipt only. Affirmed.

EDITOR'S ANALYSIS: In this case, Olmstead (P) merely substituted one contract for another. This novation did not sever any gain from capital. It merely altered the date of payment on an existing right to future payment. This holding applies only to cash basis taxpayers. Those on an accrued basis would have taxable income on the accrued commissions.

[For more information on annuities, see Casenote Law Outline on Federal Income Taxation, Chapter 5, § III, Income Security Investments.]

QUICKNOTES

NOVATION - The substitution of one party for another in a contract with the approval of the remaining party and discharging the obligations of the released party.

REALIZATION - General principle under which gains and losses are deemed to "exist" for income tax purposes only when "realized," referring to some event which marks the taxpayer's change of status with respect to the asset, principally as the result of sale, exchange, or disposition. A "deemed realization rule" is one wherein the tax law treats a nonrealization event as a realization event.

NOTES:

CRAMER v. COMMISSIONER
Taxpayer (D) v. IRS (P)
64 F.3d 1406 (9th Cir. 1995).

NATURE OF CASE: Appeal from assessment of penalties for tax deficiency.

FACT SUMMARY: Cramer (D) and other IMED executives profited from the purchase of their stock options and sought to have the gains classified as capital gains rather than income.

CONCISE RULE OF LAW: Stock options that do not have a readily ascertainable value at the time they are granted are not considered income at that time unless they are tranferable, immediately exercisable and not subject to restrictions.

FACTS: Cramer (D) and two other executives of IMED corporation were issued stock options between 1978 and 1981. The terms of the options provided certain vesting and transferring restrictions. The options were issued in recognition of the services the executives provided to the company and intended to induce their continued employment. Cramer (D) and the others decided to declare these options as ordinary income (with a value of zero) at the time of the grant, even though the stock was not publicly traded, so that the options would receive capital gains treatment in the future if they were exercised. However, an IRS regulation provided that an option must have a readily ascertainable fair market value" to treat it the way Cramer (D) did. In 1982, IMED was purchased by a larger company and Cramer's (D) stock options became worth $26 million. Cramer's (D) 1982 tax return reported nearly all of this money as a long-term capital gain and reported a basis of $7 million. The IRS (P) audited the return and determined that the option sales produced income, not capital gain, in 1982 and calculated a deficiency. It also assessed penalties for intentional disregard of the rules and substantial understatement of tax. Cramer (D) appealed.

ISSUE: Are stock options that do not have a readily ascertainable value at the time they are granted considered income unless they are tranferable, immediately exercisable and not subject to restrictions?

HOLDING AND DECISION: Yes. Stock options that do not have a readily ascertainable value at the time they are granted are not tranferable, immediately exercisable and subject to restrictions may not be considered income at the time of issuance. There is no dispute that the stock options at issue here had no readily ascertainable value, were not transferable, exercisable and were restricted. Thus, there is no doubt that Cramer (D) violated the regulations by declaring them as capital gains in 1982. However, Cramer (D) insists that the regulation is an invalid interpretation of the applicable statute. Since the regulation is not plainly inconsistent or an unreasonable interpretation of the statute, it is not invalid. Furthermore, the legislative history adds no support for Cramer's (D) position. Therefore, the stock option sale should have been treated as ordinary income for 1982 and the tax deficiency finding was proper. Additionally, the penalty imposed was proper because Cramer (D) chose to ignore the regulation rather than challenge it in the proper way. Affirmed.

EDITOR'S ANALYSIS: The court also upheld the penalty for substantial underpayment. The decision found that Cramer's (D) position did not have substantial authority and that the misrepresentations in the original tax return appeared designed to avoid audit. The court particularly noted that there had been a claimed basis for the options that was completely fabricated.

UNITED STATES v. DAVIS
Federal government (D) v. Stockholder (P)
370 U.S. 65 (1962).

NATURE OF CASE: Appeal from Court of Claims.

FACT SUMMARY: Davis (P) transferred 1,000 shares of stock to his wife in full settlement of all claims she might have.

CONCISE RULE OF LAW: The transfer of property pursuant to a marital settlement agreement is a taxable event. Taxes are computed based on the fair market value of the property at the time of transfer.

FACTS: Davis (P) separated from his wife. He transferred 1,000 shares of stock to her as full settlement of all her rights in his property. Under Delaware law she had no active interest in the ownership, management, or control of Davis' (P) property. Her only rights were inchoate including dower and intestate succession. The Commissioner (D) assessed a tax on the transfer. David (P) appealed to the Court of Claims on the basis that this was really a division of property between co-owners and, if this was found not to be the case, it would result in totally different tax treatment between taxpayers in community and noncommunity property states. The Court of Claims reversed the Commissioner (D) on the basis that the settlement might be a taxable event, but the gain realized thereby could not be determined since the wife's marital rights cannot be valuated. Because of a split in the circuits, certiorari was granted.

ISSUE: Is the transfer of property pursuant to a marital settlement agreement a taxable event?

HOLDING AND DECISION: (Clark, J.) Yes. There is no question that § 61(a) is intended to tax the economic gain on the stock. The question is should it be taxed to David (P) now or taxed when his wife disposes of it. Sections 1001 and 1002 state that gains from dealings in property are to be taxed upon "sale or other disposition." The taxpayer's argument that the transaction is akin to a non-taxable division of property between co-owners cannot be sustained. Davis' (P) wife under Delaware law has no current right to ownership, management, or control of his property. She must survive Davis (P) for her rights to ripen into ownership. Having determined that the transaction is a taxable event, we must decide the measurement of the taxable gain realized. Taxable gain is equal to the value of the property received minus the adjusted basis in the property given up. Davis (P) received a release of all his wife's claims to his property. When parties bargain at arm's length, it is presumed that the properties exchanged are of equal value. This being the case, Davis (P) received property equal to the fair market value of the stock he gave to his wife. Davis (P) should be taxed on this amount, less the original purchase price of the stock. The decision of the Commissioner (D) is affirmed.

EDITOR'S ANALYSIS: Revenue Ruling 67-221, 1967-2 C.B. 63 states that the wife takes the fair market value of the property at the time of transfer as her basis. No gain or loss is taxed to the wife. A division of community property is a nontaxable event, but if one party takes substantially all of the community property and gives the spouse a cash settlement, the transaction will be considered a sale of the spouse's half interest.

[For more information on exchanges between related parties, see Casenote Law Outline on Federal Income Taxation, Chapter 4, § IV, Recognition of Gains and Losses.]

QUICKNOTES

ADJUSTED BASIS - The occurrence of events with respect to an asset that require a corresponding increase or decrease in the value a taxpayer assigns to the costs expended in acquiring that asset, to reflect the occurrence of those events.

COMMUNITY PROPERTY - Property owned jointly by both spouses during a marriage, and which both spouses have equal rights of control over.

FAIR MARKET VALUE - The price of particular property or goods that a buyer would offer and a seller accept in the open market, following full disclosure.

NOTES:

FARID-ES-SULTANEH v. COMMISSIONER

Future wife of company owner (P) v. IRS (D)

160 F.d. 812 (d. Cir. 1947).

NATURE OF CASE: Appeal from judgment of tax deficiency.

FACT SUMMARY: Farid-es-Sultaneh (P) received stock from her future husband under an antenuptial agreement whereby, in exchange for the stock, she released all her rights for support and any interests she would obtain in his property.

CONCISE RULE OF LAW: In an antenuptial agreement, shares of stock received from one who lacked donative intent and given in exchange for a fair consideration are not a gift under I.R.C. § 1015(a).

FACTS: Farid-es-Sultaneh (P) and her future husband entered into an antenuptial agreement pursuant to which she was to receive shares of stock in the husband's company, for which she relinquished all right to support and any inchoate interests in his property. The husband's cost basis in the stock was about $0.16 per share, which would become her basis if the stock was a gift within § 1015(a). Since the husband was worth more than $400 million, her inchoate interests in his property were worth more than the value of the stock to be transferred to her. If Farid-es-Sultaneh (P) had purchased the stock for the value of her inchoate interest, she could use as a basis $10 per share for determining gains or losses. The Commissioner (D) determined that the arrangement lacked consideration and, thus, constituted a gift to Farid-es-Sultaneh (P) under I.R.C. § 1015(a), that the basis of the shares was their original purchase price, and that a deficiency was due on the amount unreported (the difference between the original basis and the amount for which the stock was sold). Farid-es-Sultaneh (P) petitioned the tax court, which upheld the Commissioner's (D) ruling. Farid-es-Sultaneh (P) appealed, arguing that consideration existed for the transfer to be taken out of the gift requirements of § 1015(a).

ISSUE: In an antenuptial agreement, are shares of stock received from one who lacked donative intent and given in exchange for a fair consideration a gift under I.R.C. § 1015(a)?

HOLDING AND DECISION: (Chase, J.) No. In an antenuptial agreement, shares of stock received from one who lacked donative intent and given in exchange for a fair consideration are not a gift under I.R.C. § 1015(a). The tax court, in holding the stock was a gift, relied on Wemyss v. Commissioner and Merrill v. Fahs, where the term "consideration" was determined to not include the value of inchoate property under similar factual circumstances. However, both cases arose under code provisions dealing with estate and gift tax. Even though those statutes were amended to limit the definition of consideration, they are not controlling when dealing with the issue of gifts under the income tax provisions [§ 1015(a)]. Thus, although the transfer here may not have been for adequate consideration under the estate and gift tax provisions, it was for adequate consideration under § 1015(a). This is supported by the legislative history of § 1015(a), which shows that Congress was attempting to close a loophole whereby the donee would use as a basis the value at the time of transfer, and, thus, any increase in value while held by the donor would not be taxed. By requiring a donee to take a basis equal to his donor's basis, § 1015(a) affected only net taxable income and did not attempt to generate a greater amount of tax on transfers, which could be taxed under the estate and gift tax provisions. Since Farid-es-Sultaneh (P) received the stock in return for her relinquishing her rights in her husband's property, the transfer was supported by consideration and was not a gift within § 1015(a). Thus, Farid-es-Sultaneh (P) could use as a basis the cost of the stock to her. Reversed.

DISSENT: (Clark, J.) No strong reason has been advanced for not applying the same rules for determining what is a gift under different sections of the tax code. The congressional purpose would appear to be identical.

EDITOR'S ANALYSIS: Section 1012 provides that for determining realized gain or loss on the sale of property, one is to use as a basis the cost of purchasing the property. Under § 1015, when property is received as a gift, and for the purpose of determining gain on the sale of such property, one must use as a basis the basis in the hands of the donor. Thus, by concluding that Farid-es-Sultaneh (P) had purchased the stock, rather than having received it as a gift, the court allowed her to receive over $10 per share "tax-free" income. Had she instead suffered a loss on the sale of the property, then the tax consequences would probably have been the same under both sections, since § 1015 provides that for the purposes of determining loss on the sale of property received as a gift, one must use the greater of either the donor's basis or the fair market value at the time the gift is made. Since she used the fair market value of the stock in computing her gain, presumably the same basis would be used for determining loss, under both §§ 1015 and 1012.

[For more information on transfers between husband and wife, see Casenote Law Outline on Federal Income Taxation, Chapter 4, § I, Basis.]

QUICKNOTES

ANTENUPTIAL AGREEMENT - An agreement entered into by two individuals, in contemplation of their impending marriage, in order to determine their rights and interests in property upon dissolution or death.

BASIS - The value assigned to a taxpayer's costs incurred as the result of acquiring an asset and used to compute tax amounts towards the transactions in which that asset is involved.

GIFT - A transfer of property to another person that is voluntary and which lacks consideration.

INCOME - Money or value earned or otherwise received as a benefit.

DIEZ-ARGUELLES v. COMMISSIONER
Divorced mother (P) v. IRS (D)
48 T.C.M. 496 (1984).

NATURE OF CASE: Review of decision denying deductions for unpaid child support.

FACT SUMMARY: Diez-Arguelles (P) sought review of the Commissioner's (D) decision disallowing her deductions for money due from her husband for child support as a nonbusiness bad debt.

CONCISE RULE OF LAW: Amounts due to a taxpayer for child support are not deductible under I.R.C. § 166 as a nonbusiness bad debt.

FACTS: Diez-Arguelles (P) was divorced in 1972, and pursuant to the divorce decree, she was to receive $300 a month in child support from her husband. By 1978, her ex-husband was $4,325 behind; in 1979, he fell another $3,000 behind. Over the years Diez-Arguelles (P) had tried unsuccessfully to collect these amounts. On her tax returns, she treated these amounts as bad nonbusiness debts, deducting these amounts from her gross income as a short-term capital loss. The Commissioner (D) disallowed both deductions, and Diez-Arguelles (P) sought review of this determination.

ISSUE: Are amounts due to a taxpayer for child support deductible under I.R.C. § 166 as a nonbusiness bad debt?

HOLDING AND DECISION: No. Amounts due to a taxpayer for child support are not deductible under I.R.C. § 166 as a nonbusiness bad debt. Nonbusiness bad debts are deductible only to the extent of the taxpayer's basis in the debts. Payments for maintenance have been found nondeductible as a nonbusiness bad debt since the taxpayer had no basis in the debt. The argument that Diez-Arguelles (P) is out-of-pocket for those expenses found uncollectible has been considered and rejected. Cases supporting dictum that a taxpayer might have a basis in a debt up to the amount that the taxpayer has expended from her own capital or income for child support are distinguishable. Sustained.

EDITOR'S ANALYSIS: The Tax Court in the present case summarily dismisses the "out-of-pocket" claim of Diez-Arguelles (P), even though it is clear that her disposable income was diminished to the extent that she had to provide for the child support. The decision does not seem terribly consistent with other deductions allowed for the support of children and places a heavy burden on a taxpayer who may not be able to bear it.

[For more information on debt discount, see Casenote Law Outline on Federal Income Taxation, Chapter 4, § III, Realization.]

QUICKNOTES

GROSS INCOME - The total income earned by an individual or business.

NOTES:

GEORGIA SCHOOL BOOK DEPOSITORY v. COMMISSIONER

Book broker (P) v. IRS (D)
1 T.C. 463 (1943).

NATURE OF CASE: Action for a redetermination of a deficiency assessment.

FACT SUMMARY: Georgia School Book Depository (Depository) (P) contended that its brokerage fees were not earned until payment and that payment would be made, therefore, the fees were not taxable until actually paid.

CONCISE RULE OF LAW: Under the accrual basis of taxpayer accounting when the right to receive an amount becomes fixed, the right accrues rendering the amount taxable income.

FACTS: The Depository (P) was a broker which received an 8% commission on all books purchased through it by the State of Georgia. It worked under an accrual method of accounting, and would receive books from the publisher and hold them in trust for the state, which would order the books through the Depository (P). Payment for the books could only come from the Free Textbook Fund created by state law from excise taxes on beer. In 1938 and 1939, the Depository (P) held certain books for the state, but did not receive payment due to a lack of money in the Fund. The IRS (D) assessed a deficiency against the Depository (P), contending its brokerage fees accrued and were, therefore, taxable in these years. The Depository (P) sued for a redetermination, contending the fees were not earned until payment and that there was no accrual because there was no reasonable expectancy that payment would ever be made.

ISSUE: Does an amount due under the accrual method of accounting become taxable when the right to receive it becomes fixed?

HOLDING AND DECISION: (Kern, J.) Yes. Under the accrual method of taxpayer accounting, when the right to receive an amount becomes fixed, the right accrues, rendering the amount taxable. In this case, the Depository (P) had done everything required of it to obtain payment in the taxable years in question. It received and stored the books and then distributed them to schools. As a result, its rights to payment became fixed, and, therefore, accrued, rendering it taxable. Further, the right to payment was not precluded from accruing because of the State's failure to immediately pay. There was no reason to believe that the prosperous State of Georgia would not eventually honor its obligation once the fund became solvent. Consequently, the payments accrued within the taxable years, rendering the Depository (P) liable for the taxes thereon. Judgment for the IRS (D).

EDITOR'S ANALYSIS: This case applies the "all events" test applicable in determining when accrual occurs. This test was first articulated in United States v. Anderson, 269 U.S. 422 (1939), in which it was held that an expense was deductible only in the year when all events which allow a determination of the amount of the liability occur. The test is codified in Regs. § 1.446-1(c)(1)(ii), as it applies to accrual of income, and Regs. § 1.461-1(a)(2) as it applies to expenses.

[For more information on the accrual method of accounting, see Casenote Law Outline on Federal Income Taxation, Chapter 8, § II, Tax Accounting Methods.]

QUICKNOTES

ACCRUAL BASIS - A method of calculating taxable income based on the time at which certain events have become fixed, including the right to receive that income, the deductions to which the taxpayer has been subject to, and the obligation to pay tax owed, regardless of when the taxpayer actually earned the income.

NOTES:

AMERICAN AUTOMOBILE ASSOC. v. UNITED STATES
Taxpayer (D) v. Federal government (D)
367 U.S. 687 (1961).

NATURE OF CASE: Action for refund of federal income taxes.

FACT SUMMARY: AAA (D), an accrual-basis taxpayer, reported as gross income only that portion of the total prepaid annual membership dues received during the year which ratably corresponded with the number of membership months, covered by those dues, occurring within the same year.

CONCISE RULE OF LAW: The Commissioner of the Internal Revenue Service did not abuse his discretion in determining that annual dues paid in advance by members of an accrual-basis automobile club at various times during the year may not be ratably apportioned by the club over the 12-month membership period.

FACTS: American Automobile Association (D), an accrual-basis taxpayer, reported as gross income only that portion of total prepaid annual membership dues received during the year which ratably corresponded with the number of membership months covered by those dues, occurring within the same year. This method was consistent with generally accepted commercial accounting principles and was consistent with AAA's (D) overall cost experience. The Commissioner contends that AAA (D) should have reported in its gross income for each year the entire amount of dues actually received in the taxable calendar year.

ISSUE: Should the annual dues paid in advance by members of an accrual-basis automobile club at various times during the year be reported as gross income for the year in which they were actually received?

HOLDING AND DECISION: (Clark, J.) Yes. In 1954 Congress enacted §§ 452 and 462 which specifically permitted essentially the same practice as employed by AAA (D). One year later, it repealed them. Since then, Congress has authorized the desired accounting only in the instance of prepaid subscription income and has specifically refused such authorization for automobile associations. At the very least, this indicates Congressional awareness of the problem involved here. The court must defer, where possible, to congressional procedures in the tax field. In light of existing provisions not specifically authorizing it, the Commissioner's exercise of discretion in refusing to recognize AAA's (D) accounting system was not unsound.

DISSENT: (Stewart, J.) The effect of the Court's decision is to allow the Commissioner to prevent an accrual taxpayer from making returns in accordance with an accepted and clearly valid accounting practice, and to compel AAA (D) to utilize a hybrid accounting method — a cash basis for dues and an accrual

method for all other items. To permit the Commissioner to do this is to ignore the clear statutory command that a taxpayer must be allowed to make his returns in accord with his regularly employed method of accounting, as long as that method clearly reflects his income.

EDITOR'S ANALYSIS: Accountants have frequently criticized the Treasury's attitude toward prepaid income and expense reserves. It was regarded as a great victory for "generally accepted accounting principles" when §§ 452 and 462 were enacted. When they were repealed it was strongly recommended that substitute provisions be adapted in the near future. No such general legislation has been enacted. However, following the American Automobile Assn. decision, Congress enacted § 456 to permit membership organizations to elect to spread prepaid dues over the period of their liability in the performance of services.

[For more information on prepaid income, see Casenote Law Outline on Federal Income Taxation, Chapter 8, § II, Tax Accounting Methods.]

QUICKNOTES

CASH BASIS - The value assigned to a taxpayer's costs incurred as the result of acquiring an asset and used to compute tax amounts towards the transactions in which that asset is involved.

NOTES:

NOTES

CHAPTER 4
PERSONAL DEDUCTIONS, EXEMPTIONS, AND CREDITS

QUICK REFERENCE RULES OF LAW

1. **Casualty Losses.** In order to claim a casualty loss, the loss must be due to an occurrence similar in character to a fire, storm, shipwreck, or theft. (Dyer v. Commissioner)

   [For more information on casualty losses, see Casenote Law Outline on Federal Income Taxation, Chapter 7, § II, Deductions for Personal Outlays.]

2. **Casualty Losses.** A taxpayer may be denied casualty loss deductibility if the loss is occasioned by his own actions. (Blackman v. Commissioner)

   [For more information on casualty losses, see Casenote Law Outline on Federal Income Taxation, Chapter 7, § II, Deductions for Personal Outlays.]

3. **What Is "Medical Care"?** Personal expenses incurred for medically related reasons may not be deductible. (Taylor v. Commissioner)

   [For more information on deductions for medical expenses, see Casenote Law Outline on Federal Income Taxation, Chapter 7, § II, Deductions for Personal Outlays.]

4. **What Is "Medical Care"?** I.R.C. deductions for medical expenses arise only from expenditures directly related to a taxpayer's health; and, where the reason for an expenditure is merely to compensate for the loss of one family member's services due to illness, such expenses are "family" not "medical" in nature and hence, non-deductible. (Ochs v. Commissioner)

   [For more information on the medical expense deduction, see Casenote Law Outline on Federal Income Taxation, Chapter 7, § II, Deductions for Personal Outlays.]

5. **Charitable Contributions: Gifts with Private Objectives or Benefits.** Under I.R.C. § 170, in order to receive a charitable deduction, a taxpayer must make his contribution exclusively for a public purpose in that he does not anticipate receipt of a substantial benefit in return. (Ottawa Silica Co. v. United States)

   [For more information on charitable contributions, see Casenote Law Outline on Federal Income Taxation, Chapter 7, § II, Deductions for Personal Outlays.]

6. **What is Charitable?** To qualify for tax exempt status under I.R.C. § 501(c)(3), an institution must be charitable in that its policies must not be contrary to public policy. (Bob Jones University v. United States)

   [For more information on charitable institutions, see Casenote Law Outline on Federal Income Taxation, Chapter 7, § II, Deductions for Personal Outlays.]

DYER v. COMMISSIONER
Cat owner (P) v. IRS (D)
20 T.C.M. 705 (1961).

NATURE OF CASE: Action for redetermination of a deficiency assessment.

FACT SUMMARY: The Dyers (P) attempted to claim a casualty loss for the destruction of a vase by their cat.

CONCISE RULE OF LAW: In order to claim a casualty loss, the loss must be due to an occurrence similar in character to a fire, storm, shipwreck, or theft.

FACTS: In 1955, the Dyers (P) claimed a casualty loss deduction of $100 for damages to a vase broken by their cat. The cat was in the process of having a neurotic fit, caused by an incurable disease which eventually required the cat to be destroyed. The IRS (D) disallowed the deduction and assessed a deficiency. The Dyers (P) petitioned the Tax Court for a redetermination, contending that the vase was not damaged during normal behavior of the cat and, therefore, it was deductible because it fell within the "other casualty" category in I.R.C. § 165(c)(3).

ISSUE: Must a loss be due to an occurrence similar in character to a fire, storm, shipwreck, or theft to be deductible as a casualty loss?

HOLDING AND DECISION: Yes. In order to claim a casualty loss, the loss must be due to a fire, storm, shipwreck, or theft. The breakage of ordinary household equipment or furnishings by a pet is not sufficiently analogous to a fire or other catastrophic occurrence, and, therefore, no casualty deduction can be allowed under these circumstances. The deficiency must be upheld.

EDITOR'S ANALYSIS: In 1983, the casualty deduction found in I.R.C. § 165(c)(3) was limited to allow only losses that exceed, in the aggregate for the year, 10 percent of the taxpayer's adjusted gross income. As a result, this case would never be litigated as it is too small. Some commentators criticize this case as establishing too limited a scope for the deduction. In Rev. Rul. 63-232, 1963-2 C.B. 97, the IRS ruled that damages due to termite infestation do not qualify as casualty losses. The rationale for this was that termite damage does not occur with the suddenness comparable to a fire, storm, or shipwreck.

[For more information on casualty losses, see Casenote Law Outline on Federal Income Taxation, Chapter 7, § II, Deductions for Personal Outlays.]

QUICKNOTES
ADJUSTED GROSS INCOME -Gross income reduced by the deductions listed in § 62.

BLACKMAN v. COMMISSIONER
Fire starter (P) v. IRS (D)
88 T.C. 677 (1987).

NATURE OF CASE: Review of deficiency assessment.

FACT SUMMARY: Blackman (P) attempted to claim as a casualty loss deduction, losses sustained due to a fire he set.

CONCISE RULE OF LAW: A taxpayer may be denied casualty loss deductibility if the loss is occasioned by his own actions.

FACTS: Blackman (P), angry at his wife, set fire to some of her clothes and then left the house. The clothes caused other portions of the house to ignite, and the house was destroyed by fire. Blackman (P) claimed the lost value of the house as a casualty deduction. The IRS (D) disallowed the deduction. Blackman (P) sought review in the Tax Court.

ISSUE: May a taxpayer be denied casualty loss deductibility if the loss is occasioned by his own actions?

HOLDING AND DECISION: Yes. A taxpayer may be denied casualty loss deductibility if the loss is occasioned by his own actions. A taxpayer will not be disallowed deductibility on a loss caused by his mere negligence. However, a loss occasioned by gross negligence or intent will result in non-deductibility. Here, the acts of Blackman were at least grossly negligent, if not worse. Moreover, a deduction will not be allowed where doing so will frustrate state public policy. Here, Maryland outlaws intentional destruction of property by fire, and allowing deductibility would frustrate this policy. Judgment for IRS (D).

EDITOR'S ANALYSIS: Casualty losses are covered in § 165 of the Internal Revenue Code. Generally speaking, when a loss comes within the ambit of this section it will be allowed in the year in which it occurred. These losses are deductible only if there is no insurance coverage.

[For more information on casualty losses, see Casenote Law Outline on Federal Income Taxation, Chapter 7, § II, Deductions for Personal Outlays.]

NOTES:

TAYLOR v. COMMISSIONER
Taxpayer (P) v. IRS (D)
54 T.C.M. 129 (1987).

NATURE OF CASE: Review of deficiency assessment.

FACT SUMMARY: Taylor (P) attempted to deduct gardening expenses incurred due to a medical prohibition against his doing his own gardening.

CONCISE RULE OF LAW: Personal expenses incurred for medically related reasons may not be deductible.

FACTS: Due to allergy problems, Taylor (P) was advised by his doctor not to mow the lawn. He hired someone else to do it. On his tax return, he claimed these expenses as a medical expense deduction. The IRS (D) disallowed the deduction. Taylor (P) sought review in Tax Court.

ISSUE: Are personal expenses incurred for medically related reasons deductible?

HOLDING AND DECISION: (Per Curiam) No. Personal expenses incurred for medically related reasons may not be deductible. The Tax Code provides a deduction for medical expenses. However, the general agreement among the authorities is that personal expenses which, while related to medical issues, do not fall within the common understanding of "medical care," are not deductible. This is precisely the case here, and the deduction was properly disallowed. Judgment for IRS (D).

EDITOR'S ANALYSIS: Generally speaking, personal living expenses are not deductible, per I.R.C. § 262. The Code provides for various exceptions, one of which is the medical expense exception of § 213. As the present case demonstrates, the IRS tends to construe the exceptions narrowly.

[For more information on deductions for medical expenses, see Casenote Law Outline on Federal Income Taxation, Chapter 7, § II, Deductions for Personal Outlays.]

QUICKNOTES

MEDICAL EXPENSE - A cost expended for the obtaining of medical treatment and deductible where such treatment takes place during the taxable year.

NOTES:

OCHS v. COMMISSIONER
Taxpayer (P) v. IRS (D)
195 F.2d 692 (2d Cir. 1952).

NATURE OF CASE: Appeal of disallowance of deduction.

FACT SUMMARY: Ochs (D) deducted the cost of sending his children to boarding school because his wife could not care for them while recovering from cancer surgery.

CONCISE RULE OF LAW: I.R.C. deductions for medical expenses arise only from expenditures directly related to a taxpayer's health; and, where the reason for an expenditure is merely to compensate for the loss of one family member's services due to illness, such expenses are "family" not "medical" in nature and hence, non-deductible.

FACTS: On December 10, 1943, Ochs (D) learned that his wife had cancer. After her operation, doctors informed Ochs (D) that the strain of child-raising might be too much for his wife during her recovery, so he sent their children to a boarding school until her recovery was complete in 1948. In 1946, he attempted to deduct the cost of this schooling as a medical expense under I.R.C. § 213 (which allows a deduction for extraordinary medical expenses, defined generally as those in excess of 3 percent of adjusted gross income). From a disallowance by the Commissioner, this appeal followed.

ISSUE: Are all expenses incurred as a result of illness, deductible as "medical" expenses under I.R.C. § 213?

HOLDING AND DECISION: (Hand, J.) No. I.R.C. deductions for medical expenses arise only from expenditures directly related to a taxpayer's health. Where the reason for an expenditure is merely to compensate for the loss of one family member's services due to illness, such expenses are "family", not "medical", in nature and hence non-deductible. The line between "family" and "medical" expenses is often a thin one. It is unlikely, however, that Congress intended to transform family child support expenses into medical expenses by § 213. The Commissioner's disallowance is affirmed.

DISSENT: (Frank, J.) The deduction should be allowed as a properly claimed medical expense. The true test for a "medical expense" ought to be whether it was incurred in response to the bonafide advice of a physician, as necessary to the recovery from or prevention of a specific ailment. Here, the taxpayer was acting on doctor's orders when he sent his children away to boarding school. Since the actual expenses incurred in acting on this advice are in no way unreasonable or excessive, they should have been allowed as deductions.

EDITOR'S ANALYSIS: I.R.C. § 213 provides that taxpayers may deduct any amount (if greater than 3 percent of gross income) paid "for the diagnosis, cure, mitigation, treatment, or prevention of disease, or for the purpose of affecting any structure or function of the body." Transportation and insurance costs incurred along with such expenses are also deductible. As for other questionable expenses, the test, as indicated above, is whether they are proximately related to medical care. Normally, "family" and other non-hospital living expenses are not deductible as medical expenses for sick taxpayers. This is because such expenses are normal everyday expenses which all taxpayers must bear.

[For more information on the medical expense deduction, see Casenote Law Outline on Federal Income Taxation, Chapter 7, § II, Deductions for Personal Outlays.]

NOTES:

OTTAWA SILICA CO. v. UNITED STATES
Mining company (P) v. Federal government (D)
699 F.2d 1124 (Fed. Cir. 1983).

NATURE OF CASE: Appeal from decision disallowing a charitable deduction.

FACT SUMMARY: Ottawa (P) donated a portion of its land for use of a public high school and attempted to deduct its value as a charitable contribution, even though he would benefit from the use of the land.

CONCISE RULE OF LAW: Under I.R.C. § 170, in order to receive a charitable deduction, a taxpayer must make his contribution exclusively for a public purpose in that he does not anticipate receipt of a substantial benefit in return.

FACTS: Ottawa (P), a company in the business of mining, processing and manufacturing quartzite, acquired ranch properties in California for their quartzite deposits. The deposits were located on only a portion of the lands. Subsequently, the land became valuable for residential development, and Ottawa (P) began exploring the possibility of so using it. The Oceanside School District approached Ottawa (P), asking it to donate 50 of its acres for a public high school. Knowing that in order to build the school, the district would have to build two access roads through its property which would substantially benefit the development, Ottawa (P) agreed to the donation. It then claimed the value of the land as a charitable deduction on its income tax return. The IRS (D) disallowed the deduction on the basis Ottawa (P) received a substantial benefit from the donation. Ottawa (P) sued, and the claims court affirmed. Ottawa (P) appealed.

ISSUE: May a taxpayer who anticipates receipt of a substantial benefit in return for his charitable donation claim a charitable deduction under I.R.C. § 170?

HOLDING AND DECISION: (Per Curiam) No. Under I.R.C. § 170, in order to receive a charitable deduction, a taxpayer must make his contribution exclusively for a public purpose. This public purpose intent requires that he not receive nor anticipate receiving a substantial benefit as a result of the contribution. In this case, Ottawa (P) knew that by law the District was required to construct the access roads which would necessarily run through Ottawa's (P) property. It therefore knew its donation would substantially increase the value of its land for residential development and, as a result, bestow a substantial benefit on Ottawa (P). Consequently, the charitable deduction must be disallowed. Affirmed.

EDITOR'S ANALYSIS: Some commentators argue that this case cannot be reconciled with cases involving so-called "psychic" returns wherein a charitable deduction is allowed. Those cases arise where a donor contributes to a university or like institution, in consideration of a building being named after him.

Further, in Rev. Rul. 80-77, 1980-1 C.B. 56, a charitable deduction was allowed to a taxpayer who contributed to the Girl Scouts while his daughter was a member of a local unit. These cases are seen by some as clearly analogous to the present case.

[For more information on charitable contributions, see Casenote Law Outline on Federal Income Taxation, Chapter 7, § II, Deductions for Personal Outlays.]

QUICKNOTES
CHARITABLE CONTRIBUTION - A gift of property or value given for charitable uses to a qualified organization or entity, and deductible by the grantor against his or her current tax liability.

NOTES:

BOB JONES UNIVERSITY v. UNITED STATES
University (P) v. Federal government (D)
461 U.S. 574 (1983).

NATURE OF CASE: Appeal from judgment granting a tax refund.

FACT SUMMARY: Bob Jones University (P) challenged the revocation of its tax exempt status, contending the revocation, based on the University's (P) racially discriminatory policies, violated the freedom of religion.

CONCISE RULE OF LAW: To qualify for tax exempt status under I.R.C. § 501(c)(3), an institution must be charitable in that its policies must not be contrary to public policy.

FACTS: Bob Jones University (P) and Goldsboro Christian Schools (P) were both private religious schools who were granted tax exempt status as charitable institutions under I.R.C. § 501(c)(3). Both had racially discriminatory policies. Bob Jones University (P) prohibited interracial dating or marriage and expelled or refused admission to students advocating such activities. Goldsboro (P) admitted only whites or children of racially mixed parentage if one parent were white. Both schools followed these policies based on their religious beliefs. The IRS (D) revoked the school's tax exempt status on the basis that the racially discriminatory policies were against public policy, precluding their status as charitable institutions. The schools (P) sued for tax refunds in separate suits, and the district court overturned the revocation, holding it violated the schools' (P) rights to religious freedom. The court of appeals reversed, and the schools (P) appealed.

ISSUE: Must an institution pursue policies consistent with public policy in order to qualify for tax exempt status as a charitable institution?

HOLDING AND DECISION: (Burger, J.) Yes. The purpose of the exemption for charitable institutions was to provide tax benefits to organizations serving charitable purposes. In this context, "charitable" takes on its common law meaning, which is that it is consistent with public policy. The grant of an exemption automatically renders other taxpayers indirect donors to the organization. In order to justify this forced contribution, the purposes of the donee organization must be consistent with public policy. It has long been recognized that racial discrimination, especially in education, violates accepted views of elementary justice and is contrary to public policy. As a result, these schools are in violation of public policy and cannot be tax exempt. Further, the public interest in nondiscrimination is sufficiently compelling to override any encroachment the revocation may cause upon religious freedom. Affirmed.

CONCURRENCE: (Powell, J.) Although racial discrimination clearly supports revocation in this case, not all charitable organizations must meet this public policy test. To agree that they must conform at all times to announced public policy makes such organizations merely arms of the government announcing such policies.

DISSENT: (Rehnquist, J.) Congress has not required that charitable organizations comply with anything but the requirements in the Internal Revenue Code. As there is no public policy requirement, this Court cannot create one.

EDITOR'S ANALYSIS: In 1982, the Reagan Administration offered a bill that would deny exemptions to racially discriminatory schools by amending § 501(c)(3). Within the discussion of the bill, it was agreed that a school which limited its enrollment to believers in the Jewish faith would be considered exempt even if it was located in an area where all the pupils would be white. The rationale was that no intent to discriminate existed.

[For more information on charitable institutions, see Casenote Law Outline on Federal Income Taxation, Chapter 7, § II, Deductions for Personal Outlays.]

NOTES:

NOTES

CHAPTER 5
ALLOWANCES FOR MIXED BUSINESS AND PERSONAL OUTLAYS

QUICK REFERENCE RULES OF LAW

1. **Controlling the Abuse of Business Deductions: Hobby Losses.** A taxpayer need only prove that he was motivated by an expectation of future profit regardless of the reasonableness of the expectation in operating a business in order to claim a business deduction. (Nickerson v. Commissioner)

   [For more information on prerequisites for business deductions, see Casenote Law Outline on Federal Income Taxation, Chapter 7, § I, Expenses Relating to the Production of Income as Opposed to Those Relating to Personal Consumption.]

2. **Controlling the Abuse of Business Deductions: Income Unconnected to a Trade or Business.** A taxpayer actively managing long-term personal investments for income purposes may not deduct expenses incurred therewith. (Moller v. United States)

   [For more information on business deductions, see Casenote Law Outline on Federal Income Taxation, Chapter 7, § I, Expenses Relating to the Production of Income as Opposed to Those Relating to Personal Consumption.]

3. **Controlling the Abuse of Business Deductions: Income Unconnected to a Trade or Business.** Wagering losses must be accounted for and reported separately from expenses incurred by the taxpayer in order to engage in the gambling activity. (Whitten v. Commissioner)

   [For more information on business deductions, see Casenote Law Outline on Book, Chapter 1, § I.]

4. **Controlling the Abuse of Business Deductions: Office Decoration.** A sufficient nexus must exist between expenses and the taxpayer's carrying on of his trade or business to qualify the expenses as an ordinary and necessary business deduction. (Henderson v. Commissioner)

   [For more information on necessary and ordinary business expenses, see Casenote Law Outline on Federal Income Taxation, Chapter 7, § I, Expenses Relating to the Production of Income as Opposed to Those Relating to Personal Consumption.]

5. **Travel and Entertainment Expenses: Question Presented.** A taxpayer who receives a trip from his employer primarily for his personal pleasure must include the value of the trip in his taxable income. (Rudolph v. United States)

   [For more information on travel expenses, see Casenote Law Outline on Federal Income Taxation, Chapter 7, § I, Expenses Relating to the Production of Income as Opposed to Those Relating to Personal Consumption.]

6. **Travel and Entertainment Expenses: Business Lunches.** The expenses of daily business meeting lunches among co-workers are not deductible as necessary business expenses, even though the meetings might be necessary from a business perspective. (Moss v. Commissioner)

   [For more information on business expenses, see Casenote Law Outline on Federal Income Taxation, Chapter 7, § I, Expenses Relating to the Production of Income as Opposed to Those Relating to Personal Consumption.]

7. **Travel and Entertainment Expenses: More on Entertaining Customers.** Deductions for business expenses will only be allowed when the taxpayer establishes that they were undertaken for bona fide business purposes.

(Danville Plywood Corporation v. United States)

[For more information on deductions for business expenses, see Casenote Law Outline on Federal Income Taxation, Chapter 7, § I, Expenses Relating to the Production of Income.]

8. **Child-Care Expenses.** I.R.C. § 262 states, "Except as otherwise expressly provided in this chapter, no deduction shall be allowed for personal, living, or family expenses," and, expenses which are personal in nature (applicable to human beings generally regardless of occupation), fall under this section and may not be claimed as business expenses merely because of some "indirect and tenuous" relationship with business pursuits. (Smith v. Commissioner)

[For more information on personal consumption expenses, see Casenote Law Outline on Federal Income Taxation, Chapter 7, § I, Expenses Relating to the Production of Income as Opposed to Those Relating to Personal Consumption.]

9. **Commuting Expenses.** A traveling expense is not a deductible trade or business expense unless it is necessary or appropriate to the development and pursuit of the business or trade of the taxpayer or of his employer. (Commissioner v. Flowers)

[For more information on commuting expenses, see Casenote Law Outline on Federal Income Taxation, Chapter 7, § I, Expenses Relating to the Production of Income as Opposed to Those Relating to Personal Consumption.]

10. **Commuting Expenses.** Traveling expenses may he deducted from gross income under I.R.C. § 162 only if the exigencies of trade or business require reasonable and necessary transportation and living costs. (Hantzis v. Commissioner)

[For more information on traveling expenses, see Casenote Law Outline on Federal Income Taxation, Chapter 7, § I, Expenses Relating to the Production of Income as Opposed to Those Relating to Personal Consumption.]

11. **Clothing Expenses.** Clothing cost is deductible as a business expense only if the clothing is specifically required as a condition of employment, it is not adaptable to general usage as ordinary clothing, and it is not so worn. (Pevsner v. Commissioner)

[For more information on prerequisites to deductibility, see Casenote Law Outline on Federal Income Taxation, Chapter 7, § I, Expenses Relating to the Production of Income as Opposed to Those Relating to Personal Consumption.]

12. **Legal Expenses.** The controlling test of whether a legal expense is "business" or "personal" (and hence, whether it is deductible or not under I.R.C. § 212) is whether or not the claim underlying it arises in connection with the taxpayer's profit-seeking activities. (United States v. Gilmore)

[For more information on legal expenses, see Casenote Law Outline on Federal Income Taxation, Chapter 7, § I, Expenses Relating to the Production of Income as Opposed to Those Relating to Personal Consumption.]

13. **Expenses of Education.** The cost of education may be deducted as a business expense where it maintains or improves skills required in the taxpayer's employment. (Carroll v. Commissioner)

[For more information on educational outlays, see Casenote Law Outline on Federal Income Taxation, Chapter 7, § I, Expenses Relating to the Production of Income as Opposed to Those Relating to Personal Consumption.]

NICKERSON v. COMMISSIONER
Advertising executive (P) v. IRS (D)
700 F.2d 402 (7th Cir. 1983).

NATURE OF CASE: Appeal from the disallowance of tax deductions.

FACT SUMMARY: The Tax Court disallowed Nickerson's (P) claimed business loss deductions, holding he was not motivated by profit in operating his farm.

CONCISE RULE OF LAW: A taxpayer need only prove that he was motivated by an expectation of future profit regardless of the reasonableness of the expectation in operating a business in order to claim a business deduction.

FACTS: Nickerson (P), an advertising executive, purchased a parcel of farmland as an alternative source of future income. The farm was in great disrepair, and in an effort to improve it, Nickerson (P) leased it to a tenant farmer for $20 per acre. This rent was the only income derived from the farm. Nickerson (P) visited the farm occasionally, and when he worked there he spent the majority of his time renovating and remodeling the farmhouse. He did not expect a profit from the farm for 10 years. In 1976 and 1977, he claimed deductions for losses incurred in renovating the farm. The IRS (D) disallowed the deductions and assessed a deficiency. Nickerson (P) sued for a redetermination, yet the Tax Court held he could not have sincerely believed that the farm would be profitable by spending so little time there and emphasizing the remodeling rather than crops or dairy production. On this basis, it found Nickerson (P) lacked a profit motive and disallowed the deduction. Nickerson (P) appealed.

ISSUE: In order to claim business deductions, must a taxpayer prove he had a reasonable expectation of immediate profit from the endeavor in order to show a sufficient profit motive?

HOLDING AND DECISION: (Pell, J.) No. A taxpayer need only prove that he was motivated by an expectation of future profit. This expectation need not be reasonable. In this case Nickerson (P) believed he could make a profit because his inducement to buy the farm was to provide an alternative source of income. He did not expect to make a profit for 10 years given the condition of the farm. It was reasonable for him to prepare the farm before depending on it for support. Further, Nickerson (P) sought expert advice and read trade journals to gain expertise in farming. This shows a plan to derive profit. As a result, the Tax Court's finding that Nickerson (P) was not profit motivated was clearly erroneous and must be reversed. The deductions must be allowed. Reversed.

EDITOR'S ANALYSIS: This case illustrates the common situation generally referred to as hobby losses. If Nickerson (P) had not been motivated by profit but had bought the farm for purely recreational reasons, his losses would not be deductible.

An endeavor engaged in to generate a tax loss must have no recreational motivation beyond the mere enjoyment of the pursuit. The primary purpose must be to gain a profit. It is often difficult to distinguish tax losses from hobby losses.

[For more information on prerequisites for business deductions, see Casenote Law Outline on Federal Income Taxation, Chapter 7, § I, Expenses Relating to the Production of Income as Opposed to Those Relating to Personal Consumption.]

QUICKNOTES

BUSINESS EXPENSE (DEDUCTION) - A cost incurred or amounts expended as "ordinary and necessary expenses" in the process of conducting an income-generating activity, currently deductible from a taxpayer's liability.

NOTES:

MOLLER v. UNITED STATES
Taxpayers (P) v. Federal government (D)
721 F.2d 810 (1983).

NATURE OF CASE: Appeal of nullification of deficiency assessment.

FACT SUMMARY: The Mollers (P) actively managed long-term personal investments as a source of income and sought to deduct expenses incurred therewith.

CONCISE RULE OF LAW: A taxpayer actively managing long-term personal investments for income purposes may not deduct expenses incurred therewith.

FACTS: The Mollers (P) had personal investment portfolios of over $10,000 each. Both the Mollers (P) actively managed their portfolios, spending approximately 40 hours per week keeping up with the financial markets. The investments tended to be of the long-term variety. The Mollers (P) attempted to declare as deductions the costs incurred in keeping offices in their homes. These offices were used solely for purposes pertaining to investment management. The IRS disallowed the deductions, and made a deficiency assessment. The Court of Claims held the Mollers (P) to be carrying on a business, and allowed the deductions. The IRS (D) appealed.

ISSUE: May a taxpayer actively managing long-term personal investments for income purposes deduct expenses incurred therewith?

HOLDING AND DECISION: (Kashiwa, J.) No. A taxpayer actively managing long-term personal investments for income purposes may not deduct expenses incurred therewith. The I.R.C. permits a taxpayer carrying on a business at home to deduct those expenses reasonably related to the business. The production of income is not the same thing as a business. One managing his own investments for his own benefit is not carrying on a business. He is merely investing, and the amount of time spent in performing this activity is not relevant to whether a business is being carried on. Here, the Mollers (P) merely manage their own investments, and thus were not carrying on a business. Reversed.

EDITOR'S ANALYSIS: A stockbroker or investment fund manager is, of course, carrying on a business. The court labels this sort of individual as a "trader," rather than an "investor." The most significant differences are that the trader tends to trade short-term, and does not deal exclusively with his own investments.

[For more information on business deductions, see Casenote Law Outline on Federal Income Taxation, Chapter 7, § I, Expenses Relating to the Production of Income as Opposed to Those Relating to Personal Consumption.]

WHITTEN v. COMMISSIONER
Taxpayer (D) v. IRS (P)
T.C. Memo. 1995-508.

NATURE OF CASE: Cross motions for summary judgment.

FACT SUMMARY: The Whittens (D) claimed that their expenses for traveling to Los Angeles so that Mr. Whitten (D) could participate in the television game show the "Wheel of Fortune" constituted wagering losses deductible against their winnings under §165(d).

CONCISE RULE OF LAW: Wagering losses must be accounted for and reported separately from expenses incurred by the taxpayer in order to engage in the gambling activity.

FACTS: The Whittens (D) filed a joint 1991 Federal income tax return. In February 1991 the Whittens (D) flew to Los Angeles so that Mr. Whitten (D) could participate in the "Wheel of Fortune" game show. He won three consecutive games and cash prizes totaling $14,850. He also won a 1991 Chevrolet Geo Tracker automobile. In their joint tax return the Whittens (D) reported the game show winnings as "other income" totaling $19,830 on line 22 of Form 1040. This amount represented the winnings minus expenses for the trip to Los Angeles. The Whittens (D) claimed such expenses represented "gambling losses" that may be offset directly against the "gambling winnings" gained from the show. The Commissioner (P) determined a deficiency of $582 for failure to report $1,820 in income from the game show. The Commissioner (P) contends that the $1,820 in claimed expenses constitute either non-deductible personal expenses under §262 or miscellaneous itemized deductions subject to the two percent floor of §67(b).

ISSUE: Must wagering losses be accounted for and reported separately from expenses incurred by the taxpayer in order to engage in the gambling activity?

HOLDING AND DECISION: (No judge listed.) Yes. Wagering losses must be accounted for and reported separately from expenses incurred by the taxpayer in order to engage in the gambling activity. The term "wagering losses" is not defined in either the IRC or the regulations. In Kozma v. Commissioner, the taxpayer, who was involved in the business of gambling, reported net losses with respect to his gambling business his expenses outweighed his earnings for the taxable period. There the court held that the Commissioner was correct in disallowing losses to the extent they constituted a loss from the taxpayer's gambling business. Here Whitten (D) is not in the business of gambling and he did not incur losses or expenses that exceeded his winnings. Whitten (D) erroneously believes that Kozma held that all expenses related to gambling activities might be characterized as wagering losses under §165(d). Rather, wagering losses must be accounted for and reported separately from expenses incurred in the engagement in the gambling activity. Whitten's (D) expenses are better characterized as a miscellaneous itemized deduction under §67 instead of a wagering loss under §165(d). Whitten (D) also argued that the expenses were equal to a bet or wager. This argument fails as well as it is unlikely that Congress intended casual gamblers to treat such expenses as other than miscellaneous itemized deductions or nondeductible personal expenses. Whitten's (D) motion for summary judgment denied. Summary judgment granted in favor of the Commissioner (P).

EDITOR'S ANALYSIS: Note that the result here also turns on the fact that Whitten (D) was not engaged in gambling as a profession. The term "wagering losses" as used in §165(d) is only applicable to professional gamblers and only includes those losses incurred as a result of a wagering transaction, not expenses incurred in engaging in the transaction. Kozma narrowly held that in the case of professional gamblers, the §165(d) limitation supercedes the §162(a) deduction for ordinary and necessary business expenses.

HENDERSON v. COMMISSIONER
Attorney (P) v. IRS (D)
46 T.C.M. 566 (1983).

NATURE OF CASE: Review of decision disallowing deductions.

FACT SUMMARY: Henderson (P) appealed from a decision of the Commissioner (D) disallowing the deductions she had claimed for a framed print and a plant in her office and for a parking fee to rent parking space across from her office.

CONCISE RULE OF LAW: A sufficient nexus must exist between expenses and the taxpayer's carrying on of his trade or business to qualify the expenses as an ordinary and necessary business deduction.

FACTS: Henderson (P) was employed as an attorney. She was provided with a desk and equipment and supplies necessary to conduct her practice. She bought a plant and a framed print for her office and rented a space across the street to park her car. She occasionally used her car when a car was not available. She deducted these costs as necessary and ordinary business expenses. The Commissioner (D) disallowed the deductions and issued a notice of deficiency, from which Henderson (P) appealed.

ISSUE: Must a sufficient nexus exist between expenses and the carrying on of a taxpayer's trade or business to qualify the expenses as a necessary and ordinary business expense?

HOLDING AND DECISION: Yes. A sufficient nexus must exist between expenses and the carrying on of a taxpayer's trade or business to qualify the expenses as a necessary business deduction. Even if the expense is incurred in the carrying on of business, it may be disallowed if incurred for a personal reason. It is clear that where both the business expense deduction and the personal or living expense nondeduction both apply, the latter will prevail over the former. The expenses for the plant and the print were for decoration and only tangentially aided her in the performance of her duties as an attorney. A remote or incidental connection is not enough, and there is no evidence that they were necessary or helpful. Accordingly, the deductions for these two items are disallowed.

EDITOR'S ANALYSIS: It is not clear from the opinion what happened for the deduction for the parking space. It is likely that such an expenditure, partly for Henderson's (P) personal convenience, and partly useful for the performance of her job, could be prorated and the deduction allowed for that part attributable to her carrying out her duties. If it cannot be prorated, the general rule seems to be that the predominant purpose behind the expense prevails, not necessarily the personal expense nondeduction as stated in the present case.

[For more information on necessary and ordinary business expenses, see Casenote Law Outline on Federal Income Taxation, Chapter 7, § I, Expenses Relating to the Production of Income as Opposed to Those Relating to Personal Consumption.]

NOTES:

RUDOLPH v. UNITED STATES
Insurance salesman (P) v. Federal government (D)
370 U.S. 269 (1962).

NATURE OF CASE: Appeal from the denial of a tax refund.

FACT SUMMARY: Rudolph (P) contended that the value of a trip given to him by his employer was not taxable as income.

CONCISE RULE OF LAW: A taxpayer who receives a trip from his employer primarily for his personal pleasure must include the value of the trip in his taxable income.

FACTS: Rudolph (P), by selling a predetermined amount of insurance, qualified to attend his company's convention in New York City and to take his wife along. The trip lasted one week and included one business meeting. The rest of the time, Rudolph (P) was free to do as he pleased. The entire cost of the trip was paid by his employer. The IRS (D) contended the trip was personal as it was primarily for pleasure, and therefore, included the cost in Rudolph's (P) taxable income. Rudolph (P) sued for a refund, contending it was a business trip and that he was compelled to go to ensure goodwill with his employer. The district court held that the trip was provided by the company as a bonus for good work and was primarily a pleasure trip. On this basis, the refund was denied, and Rudolph (P) appealed.

ISSUE: Must the value of a trip received by an employee for his personal pleasure be included in his taxable income?

HOLDING AND DECISION: (Per curiam) Yes. A taxpayer who receives a trip from his employer primarily for his personal pleasure must include the value of the trip in his taxable income. In this case, the district court found as a matter of fact that the primary purpose of the trip was to give a bonus or reward to Rudolph (P) to use for his personal pleasure. Because these findings are not clearly erroneous, they must be upheld. As a result, the value was properly included in Rudolph's (P) income and the refund properly denied. Affirmed.

CONCURRENCE: (White, J.) Because this was essentially a pleasure trip, its cost was not deductible by Rudolph (P) as an ordinary and necessary business expense.

DISSENT: (Douglas, J.) The payment of expenses to a professional convention cannot be considered income. This is in no way compensation for services rendered. Further, the cost was deductible by the employer.

EDITOR'S ANALYSIS: Rev. Rul. 76-453 holds that a person may deduct the cost of food and lodging when it is necessary to travel on business. Also the cost of getting there and back is deductible. This situation poses few problems in analysis. It does where, as in this case, the trip is mixed with business and pleasure. In such a case, courts usually allow the deduction if the primary purpose of the trip is business in nature.

[For more information on travel expenses, see Casenote Law Outline on Federal Income Taxation, Chapter 7, § I, Expenses Relating to the Production of Income as Opposed to Those Relating to Personal Consumption.]

NOTES:

MOSS v. COMMISSIONER
Attorney (P) v. IRS (D)
758 F.2d 211 (7th Cir. 1985).

NATURE OF CASE: Appeal from decision disallowing tax deductions.

FACT SUMMARY: Moss (P) appealed from a Tax Court decision disallowing a tax deduction on his share of his firm's daily business meeting lunch expenses, contending that the business nature of the daily lunch would qualify the lunch expense for necessary business expense treatment.

CONCISE RULE OF LAW: The expenses of daily business meeting lunches among coworkers are not deductible as necessary business expenses, even though the meetings might be necessary from a business perspective.

FACTS: Moss (P) was a partner in a small law firm specializing in trial work. The members of the firm met daily for lunch at Angelo's, a restaurant convenient for their practice. At the meeting, cases were discussed with the head of the firm, and the firm's trial schedule was worked out at these lunch meetings. These meetings were necessary as each member of the firm carried an enormous caseload, requiring the members of the firm to spend most of their day in court. Thus, lunch was the most convenient meeting time, as the courts were then in recess. There was no suggestion that the attorneys dawdled over lunch, or that the restaurant chosen was extravagant. Moss (P) sought to deduct his share of the lunch expenses as a necessary business expense. The Commissioner (D) took the position that the lunch expenses were not deductible. The Tax Court agreed with the Commissioner (D) and disallowed the deductions. From this decision Moss (P) appealed.

ISSUE: Are the expenses of daily business meeting lunches among coworkers deductible as necessary business expenses where the meetings would be considered necessary from a business perspective?

HOLDING AND DECISION: (Posner, J.) Yes. The expenses of daily business meeting lunches among coworkers are not deductible as necessary business expenses, even though the meetings might be necessary from a business perspective. Given the unique nature of the firm's practice there is not much dispute that the meetings themselves were necessary for the smooth functioning of the firm, and that lunch was the most convenient time to hold such meetings. Meals are deductible when they are necessary and ordinary business expenses. There is a natural reluctance to allow deductions for expenses both business and personal in nature and because the meal deduction is allowed, the Commissioner (D) requires that the meal expense be a real business necessity. The considerations involved with business meetings with coworkers are different than where the meetings are among coworkers. In client entertainment situations, the business objective, to be fully achieved, requires the sharing of a meal. In the present situation, the meal was not an organic part of the meeting, even though the meetings were necessary from a business perspective and lunch was the most convenient time for the meeting. In evaluating cases like this, decisions must be based on the frequency of the meetings and the individual degree and circumstance of the luncheon meetings sought to be deducted. In this case, however, the lunches, not being an organic part of the business purpose of the meetings, are not deductible. Affirmed.

EDITOR'S ANALYSIS: The current state of deductibility for expenses as long as a plausible business connection can be demonstrated is particularly unjust to a majority of taxpayers, who cannot take advantage of such deductions by virtue of their employment. Such inequities are most apparent in connection with the deductibility of various entertainment functions, such as tickets to sporting and theatrical events, which involve a significant personal component, and allow a personal subsidy to those in a position to take advantage of business deductions.

[For more information on business expenses, see Casenote Law Outline on Federal Income Taxation, Chapter 7, § I, Expenses Relating to the Production of Income as Opposed to Those Relating to Personal Consumption.]

NOTES:

DANVILLE PLYWOOD CORPORATION v. UNITED STATES

Employer (P) v. IRS (D)

899 F.2d 3 (1990).

NATURE OF CASE: Appeal from denial of tax deduction.

FACT SUMMARY: In Danville's (P) action against the Government (D), challenging the Tax Commissioner's decision to disallow it a deduction for its alleged business-related expenses, the claims court agreed with the Commissioner.

CONCISE RULE OF LAW: Deductions for business expenses will only be allowed when the taxpayer establishes that they were undertaken for bona fide business purposes.

FACTS: Buchanan, the president of Danville (P), hosted a Super Bowl trip, inviting mainly customer representatives and their spouses along with, to a lesser degree, his employees and their spouses. During the trip, Buchanan and his employees briefly met with these customers to informally discuss Danville (P) business products during a Super Bowl-eve dinner, where some of these products were displayed in an area adjacent to the dining area. Later, Danville (P) claimed this trip as a business deduction, which was denied by the Commissioner. Danville (P) brought an action against the Government (D) in claims court to contest the Commissioner's determination. Notwithstanding this challenge, however, the claims court held that the expenses incurred were not for a bona fide business purpose and thus not deductible. Danville (P) appealed.

ISSUE: Will deductions for business expenses only be allowed when a taxpayer establishes that they were undertaken for bona fide business purposes?

HOLDING AND DECISION: Yes. Deductions for business expenses will only be allowed when a taxpayer establishes that they were undertaken for bona fide business purposes. This rule merely restates the statutory principle as laid down in § 162 of the Internal Revenue Code. This principle states, in effect, that an expense must be an ordinary and necessary business expense in order to be deductible. Moreover, if the Commissioner, in applying § 162, determines that a business expense is not deductible, then the taxpayer bears the burden of providing evidence to support a contrary finding. In the instant case, Danville (P) failed to demonstrate that the trip was undertaken for bona fide business purposes. Accordingly, Danville (P) was not entitled to a deduction for this trip. Affirmed.

EDITOR'S ANALYSIS: Had Danville (P) simply given its employees cash equal to the cost of the travel and entertainment, the expense would clearly have been deducted as salary. Indeed, had Danville (P) given its employees (and their relatives) a free vacation and reported that expense as salary to the employees, it is virtually certain it would have been deductible under § 162. Seen from this perspective, the "offending" aspect of the Super Bowl trip was not the deduction to the employer but the fact that the employer did not report the value of the travel and entertainment as income and that the employees did not pay tax on that income.

[For more information on deductions for business expenses, see Casenote Law Outline on Federal Income Taxation, Chapter 7, § I, Expenses Relating to the Production of Income.]

QUICKNOTES

BUSINESS EXPENSE - A cost incurred or amounts expended as "ordinary and necessary expenses" in the process of conducting an income-generating activity, currently deductible from a taxpayer's liability

NOTES:

SMITH v. COMMISSIONER
Parents (P) v. IRS (D)
40 B.T.A. 1038 (1939).

NATURE OF CASE: Appeal of disallowance of deduction for childcare.

FACT SUMMARY: The Smiths (P), husband and wife, attempted to claim a business deduction for childcare while Mrs. Smith (P) was working.

CONCISE RULE OF LAW: I.R.C. § 262 states, "Except as otherwise expressly provided in this chapter, no deduction shall be allowed for personal, living, or family expenses," and, expenses which are personal in nature (applicable to human beings generally regardless of occupation), fall under this section and may not be claimed as business expenses merely because of some "indirect and tenuous" relationship with business pursuits.

FACTS: The Smiths (P), husband and wife, claimed a deduction for childcare (nursemaids), which expense was incurred so as to enable Mrs. Smith (P) to take a job. When the Commissioner (D) disallowed the deduction, the Smiths (P) objected. From judgment for the Commissioner, (D), the Smiths (P) appealed, claiming that the deduction should be allowed as a business expense since "but for" the childcare, Mrs. Smith (P) could not work.

ISSUE: May an expense be properly classified as a business expense (i.e., deductible) because it relieves a taxpayer of some personal or family responsibilities which would otherwise prevent that taxpayer from working?

HOLDING AND DECISION: (Opper, J.) No. I.R.C. § 262 states, "Except as otherwise expressly provided in this chapter, no deduction shall be allowed for personal, living, or family expenses," and, expenses which are personal in nature (applicable to human beings generally regardless of occupation), fall under this section and may not be claimed as business expenses merely because of some "indirect and tenuous" relationship with business pursuits. It is true that some normally personal expenses may become business expenses because their connection with business pursuits have come to be a matter of "common acceptance and universal experience" (e.g., entertainment). The so-called "working wife" is not such a matter, however, and her expenses for nursemaids are not deductible.

EDITOR'S ANALYSIS: The harsh and archaic position of this case toward childcare has been supplanted by the 1971 Revenue Act. Pursuant to that Act, up to $400 a month in childcare is now permitted to families in which both parents (or one parent if both parents are not living together) work. Note, however, that § 262 is still in effect (childcare is merely exempted from it). It is still true that personal expenses are not deductible. As such, work clothes, for example, which are suitable for ordinary wear are not deductible but special clothes (work gloves, helmets, etc.) are. Military uniforms worn by active duty officers are not deductible because they take the place of ordinary clothes, but uniforms for part-time reserve personnel are.

[For more information on personal consumption expenses, see Casenote Law Outline on Federal Income Taxation, Chapter 7, § I, Expenses Relating to the Production of Income as Opposed to Those Relating to Personal Consumption.]

NOTES:

COMMISSIONER v. FLOWERS
IRS (D)v. Attorney (P)
326 U.S. 465 (1945).

NATURE OF CASE: Action challenging the determination of a tax deficiency.

FACT SUMMARY: Having accepted a job with a company headquartered in Mobile, with the intention of continuing to live in Jackson, Flowers (P) attempted to deduct the resulting travel and living expenses.

CONCISE RULE OF LAW: A traveling expense is not a deductible trade or business expense unless it is necessary or appropriate to the development and pursuit of the business or trade of the taxpayer or of his employer.

FACTS: A lawyer who had done work for and was involved with Gulf, Mobile & Ohio Railroad, headquartered in Mobile, agreed to accept the position of general counsel if he could continue to live in Jackson. Being able to do most of his work where he wanted, Flowers (P) made 33 trips between the two cities in 1939 and 40 trips in 1940. Flowers (P) attempted to deduct these travel expenses as trade or business expenses under I.R.C. § 162(a)(2). Deficiencies were assessed when the deductions were disallowed. The Tax Court upheld the Commissioner (D) but was reversed on appeal.

ISSUE: Can travel expenses be deducted as trade or business expense if they are not necessary or appropriate to the development and pursuit of the business or trade of the taxpayer or of his employ?

HOLDING AND DECISION: (Murphy, J.) No. One of the conditions required before a travel expense can be deducted as a trade or business expense is that it was necessary or appropriate to the development and pursuit of the business or trade of the taxpayer or of his employer. The other two conditions are that it was a reasonable and necessary business expense, and that it was incurred "while away from home." This case is disposed of quickly because it fails to meet the first condition mentioned. The facts clearly demonstrate that the expenses were not incurred in the pursuit of the business of Flowers' (P) employer but were incurred solely as the result of Flowers' (P) desire to maintain a home in Jackson while working in Mobile. Reversed.

DISSENT: (Rutledge, J.) The only question this case truly presents is whether the expenses were "incurred away from home," and they were. This is different from the regular commuting case, where a taxpayer works within a distance permitting a daily journey and return.

EDITOR'S ANALYSIS: In one case, the IRS acted to lessen some of the harsher implications of this case. It ruled in favor of allowing a deduction for travel expenses incurred by a construction worker whose trade or business consisted of a series of temporary employments. Revenue Ruling 60-189, 1960-1 C.B. 60.

[For more information on commuting expenses, see Casenote Law Outline on Federal Income Taxation, Chapter 7, § I, Expenses Relating to the Production of Income as Opposed to Those Relating to Personal Consumption.]

NOTES:

HANTZIS v. COMMISSIONER
Law student (P) v. IRS (D)
638 F.2d 248 (1st Cir.); cert. denied, 452 U.S. 962 (1981).

NATURE OF CASE: Appeal from allowance of deduction.

FACT SUMMARY: Hantzis (P), living in Boston, deducted the cost of traveling to New York and maintaining an apartment there while working as a summer law clerk and the Commissioner (D) disallowed the deduction.

CONCISE RULE OF LAW: Traveling expenses may he deducted from gross income under I.R.C. § 162 only if the exigencies of trade or business require reasonable and necessary transportation and living costs.

FACTS: Hantzis (P) lived with her husband in Boston, where she attended law school. Unable to secure employment as a law clerk for the summer in Boston, she moved to New York City and rented an apartment there so as to work for a New York law firm. She visited Boston only intermittently in the 10 weeks of employment. Hantzis (P) deducted the travel expenses and the cost of maintaining the apartment from their income tax form, the Commissioner (D) disallowed the deduction, the trial court overruled him, and the Commissioner (D) appealed.

ISSUE: May traveling expenses be deducted from gross income under I.R.C. § 162 only if the exigencies of trade or business require reasonable and necessary transportation and living costs?

HOLDING AND DECISION: (Campbell, J.) Yes. If no business exigency dictates the location of the taxpayer's usual residence, then the mere fact of his taking employment elsewhere cannot supply a compelling business reason for continuing to maintain that residence. Only a taxpayer who lives in one place, works in another, and has business ties to both is entitled to deduct traveling expenses as business expenses. Hantzis (P) had no business contact with Boston and her extended stay in New York requires a finding that New York was her "home" for purposes of I.R.C. § 162. Traveling expenses may be deducted from gross income under I.R.C. § 162 only if the exigencies of trade or business require reasonable and necessary transportation and living costs. Reversed.

CONCURRENCE: (Keeton, J.) Hantzis (P) was not required by her trade or business to maintain two places of residence. She earned no income in Boston and, thus, had no business ties to that city. The deduction was properly disallowed.

EDITOR'S ANALYSIS: If Hantzis (P) had been holding down a job in Boston and then been sent by her employer to New York, her unreimbursed expenses would have been deductible. This is the situation contemplated by the statute. The court found some difficulty in defining "home" and did no better than past cases, but was at least able to find that Boston was not Hantzis' (P) home if all of her income came from New York, and Boston played no role in her business or trade.

[For more information on traveling expenses, see Casenote Law Outline on Federal Income Taxation, Chapter 7, § I, Expenses Relating to the Production of Income as Opposed to Those Relating to Personal Consumption.]

QUICKNOTES
GROSS INCOME - The total income earned by an individual or business.

TRAVEL EXPENSE - A cost expended for activities attendant to travel while conducting business rather than pleasure; may be treated as a business expense, which may be deductible.

NOTES:

PEVSNER v. COMMISSIONER
Employee (P) v. IRS (D)
628 F.2d 467 (5th Cir. 1980).

NATURE OF CASE: Appeal from decision upholding a business expense deduction.

FACT SUMMARY: Pevsner (P) contended that because clothing she was required to purchase and wear in her employment was not consistent with her personal lifestyle, she could deduct their cost as a business expense.

CONCISE RULE OF LAW: Clothing cost is deductible as a business expense only if the clothing is specifically required as a condition of employment, it is not adaptable to general usage as ordinary clothing, and it is not so worn.

FACTS: Pevsner (P) was employed as the manager of the Sakowitz Yves St. Laurent Rive Gauche Boutique, which sold only women's clothes designed by Yves St. Laurent, a famous designer. The clothing was highly fashionable and expensively priced. Pevsner (P) was required as a condition of her employment to wear Yves St. Laurent clothes while working. She purchased $1,381.91 worth of the clothes and wore them exclusively at work. At home she lived a very simple life and the clothes would not be consistent with this lifestyle. She deducted the cost of clothes as a business expense, yet the IRS (D) disallowed the deduction contending she could have worn the clothes away from work and her choice not to was irrelevant to the deductibility of the clothes. The Tax Court allowed the deduction, and the IRS (D) appealed.

ISSUE: Is clothing cost a deductible business expense only if the clothing is specifically required as a condition of employment, it is not adaptable to general usage as ordinary clothing, and it is not so worn?

HOLDING AND DECISION: (Johnson, J.) Yes. Clothing cost is deductible as a business expense only if the clothing is specifically required as a condition of employment, it is not adaptable to general use as ordinary clothing, and it is not so worn. In this case, the clothing was clearly a condition of employment. However, it was only by choice that Pevsner (P) failed to wear the clothing away from work. This element must be determined by an objective test. If a deduction were allowed on the subjective attitude of the taxpayer, no workable guidelines for the deduction could be developed. Therefore, because the clothing was adaptable to ordinary use the deduction cannot be allowed. Reversed.

EDITOR'S ANALYSIS: The use of this objective test in determining whether clothing is deductible under §§ 162 and 262 avoids an unfair application of the deduction. The subjective test would allow similarly situated taxpayers to be treated differently according to their lifestyle and socio-economic level. The objective test allows the greatest level of fairness to the greatest number of taxpayers.

_____

[For more information on prerequisites to deductibility, see Casenote Law Outline on Federal Income Taxation, Chapter 7, § I, Expenses Relating to the Production of Income as Opposed to Those Relating to Personal Consumption.]

NOTES:

UNITED STATES v. GILMORE
Federal government (P) v. Taxpayer (D)
372 U.S. 39 (1963).

NATURE OF CASE: Appeal of Tax Court decision.

FACT SUMMARY: Gilmore (D) deducted legal expenses incurred in connection with divorce proceedings brought by his wife.

CONCISE RULE OF LAW: The controlling test of whether a legal expense is "business" or "personal" (and hence, whether it is deductible or not under I.R.C. § 212) is whether or not the claim underlying it arises in connection with the taxpayer's profit-seeking activities.

FACTS: Gilmore (D) expended several thousand dollars over two years in order to defeat his wife's suit for divorce and alimony. Both years, he attempted to deduct these legal expenses on his tax return pursuant to I.R.C. § 212 which allows deductions for "ordinary and necessary expense . . . incurred during the taxable year . . . for the . . . conservation . . . of property held for the production of income." Gilmore's (D) position was that, without his divorce's resulting expenses, his wife would be able to materially cut into his income-producing assets (three car dealerships) through alimony. The Commissioner disallowed the deduction but the Court of Claims allowed it. This appeal followed.

ISSUE: May legal expenses be deducted as ordinary and necessary to the production of income (§ 212) merely because the consequences of losing the action involved would cut into profit- making resources?

HOLDING AND DECISION: (Harlan, J.) No. The controlling test of whether a legal expense is "business" or "personal" (and, hence, whether it is deductible under I.R.C. § 212) is whether or not the claim underlying it arises in connection with the taxpayer's profit-seeking activities. It is true that losing a suit may impair profit-making potential by depleting resources, but, permitting this to be the basis of a business deduction would stretch Congressional intent in passing § 212 too far. Here, Gilmore's (D) legal expenses arose from personal not business problems. His deductions were, therefore, improper. Judgment reversed.

EDITOR'S ANALYSIS: This case points up the general rule that legal expenses incurred in divorce proceedings, even where extensive business holdings are involved in property settlements, are personal, not business, in nature. Some minor exceptions do exist, however. Legal fees for advice regarding the tax consequences of a divorce (as all expenses incurred in connection with the determination of any tax problem) are deductible. Furthermore, a wife may deduct any legal fees incurred in connection with the collection of her alimony income, since such is treated on a par with the husband's profit-seeking

activities. Note, that § 212 makes available to the individual investor the same type of expense deduction which § 162 allows to businessmen (*i.e.*, ordinary and necessary expenses incurred for the production of income).

[For more information on legal expenses, see Casenote Law Outline on Federal Income Taxation, Chapter 7, § I, Expenses Relating to the Production of Income as Opposed to Those Relating to Personal Consumption.]

NOTES:

CARROLL v. COMMISSIONER
Police officer (P) v. IRS (D)
418 F.2d 91 (7th Cir. 1969).

NATURE OF CASE: Appeal from disallowance of deduction for educational expenses.

FACT SUMMARY: Carroll (P), a police officer, attempted to deduct the cost of his prelaw studies as an expense relative to improving his job skills.

CONCISE RULE OF LAW: The cost of education may be deducted as a business expense where it maintains or improves skills required in the taxpayer's employment.

FACTS: Carroll (P), a police officer, enrolled in DePaul University in preparation for the study of law, majoring in philosophy. He enrolled in six courses: two English, two philosophy, one history, and one political science. He deducted the cost of his enrollment, contending it was an expense relative to improving his job skills. The IRS (D) disallowed the deduction, contending the classes were not sufficiently related to his employment to be deductible. The Tax Court affirmed, and Carroll (P) appealed.

ISSUE: Can the cost of a general college education be deducted as a business expense?

HOLDING AND DECISION: (Castle, J.) No. The cost of an education may be deducted as a business expense only where it maintains or improves skills required in the taxpayer's employment. While a general college education clearly would improve Carroll's (P) performance as a police officer, there is an insufficient relationship between the subjects studied and the skills required of a policeman to find that the classes improved or maintained the skills. As a results, the cost could not be deducted. Affirmed.

EDITOR'S ANALYSIS: Not all costs of education are nondeductible. A course in industrial psychology would clearly be deductible to an industrial psychologist as would continuing legal education be to an attorney. These are allowable deductions even though they may lead to advanced degrees or new job opportunities. The difference between deductible and nondeductible costs of education is no longer the primary purpose test. Rather it is the logical connection in subject matter. The former standard — the primary purpose test — was abolished by Regs. §§ 1.162-5.

[For more information on educational outlays, see Casenote Law Outline on Federal Income Taxation, Chapter 7, § I, Expenses Relating to the Production of Income as Opposed to Those Relating to Personal Consumption.]

6

CHAPTER 6
DEDUCTIONS FOR THE COSTS OF EARNING INCOME

QUICK REFERENCE RULES OF LAW

1. **Current Expenses versus Capital Expenditures.** Where an expenditure is made with the intent that it will generate income over a period of years, it is classified as a capital expenditure and is not currently deductible as a business expense. (Encyclopaedia Britannica v. Commissioner)

   [For more information on capital expenditures, see Casenote Law Outline on Federal Income Taxation, Chapter 6, § I, Distinguishing Capital Expenditures from Expenses.]

2. **Repair and Maintenance Expenses.** A structural change which does not increase the useful life or use of a building and which is the normal method of dealing with a given problem is a "repair" for tax purposes. (Midland Empire Packing Co. v. Commissioner)

   [For more information on capital improvements, see Casenote Law Outline on Federal Income Taxation, Chapter 6, § I, Distinguishing Capital Expenditures from Expenses.]

3. **Repair and Maintenance Expenses.** Where a taxpayer incurs costs associated with the improvement of property so that the value of the property is increased, its use is prolonged, or it is fashioned for a different use, such expense is classified as a capital improvement and must be capitalized. (Norwest Corporation v. Commissioner)

   [For more information on capital expenditures, see Casenote Law Outline on Federal Income Taxation, Chapter 6, § I, Distinguishing Capital Expenditures from Expenses.]

4. **Rent Payment versus Installment Purchase.** A rental contract in which property is transferred that provides for a nominal price for renewal at termination will be treated as a contract of sale. (Starr's Estate v. Commissioner)

   [For more information on capital expenditures, see Casenote Law Outline on Federal Income Taxation, Chapter 6, § I, Distinguishing Capital Expenditures from Expenses.]

5. **Goodwill and Other Assets.** In order to be deductible, an expense must be "ordinary" in the business area practiced by the taxpayer. (Welch v. Helvering)

   [For more information on nondeductible outlays, see Casenote Law Outline on Federal Income Taxation, Chapter 7, § I, Expenses Relating to the Production of Income as Opposed to Those Relating to Personal Consumption.]

6. **"Ordinary and Necessary": Extraordinary Behavior.** Where activities giving rise to a taxpayer's legal expenses were not activities directly in the conduct of the taxpayer's trade or business, the expenses are not deductible as an ordinary and necessary business expense. (Gilliam v. Commissioner)

   [For more information on legal expenses, see Casenote Law Outline on Federal Income Taxation, Chapter 7, § I, Expenses Relating to the Production of Income as Opposed to Those Relating to Personal Consumption.]

7. **"Ordinary and Necessary": Costs of Illegal or Unethical Activities.** A deduction may not be allowed for uncompensated losses sustained during the taxable year when it would frustrate public policy. (Stephens v. Commissioner)

[For more information on deductions for business expenses, see Casenote Law Outline on Federal Income Taxation, Chapter 7, § I, Expenses Relating to the Production of Income.]

8. **The Judicial Response to Tax Shelters.** I.R.C. § 163 permits taxpayers to deduct all "interest paid. . . on indebtedness," but, where a taxpayer enters into a sham loan transaction which serves no purpose except to reduce the amount of that taxpayer's tax, such deduction will not be allowed. (Knetsch v. United States)

[For more information on deductibility of interest payments, see Casenote Law Outline on Federal Income Taxation, Chapter 7, § I, Expenses Relating to the Production of Income as Opposed to Those Relating to Personal Consumption.]

9. **The Judicial Response to Tax Shelters.** Depreciation is not predicated upon ownership of property but rather upon an investment in property. (Estate of Franklin v. Commissioner)

[For more information on acquisition indebtedness, see Casenote Law Outline on Federal Income Taxation, Chapter 4, § I, Basis.]

10. **The Alternative Minimum Tax.** The Alternative Minimum Tax is not inequitable. (Prosman v. Commissioner)

[For more information on the Alternative Minimum Tax, see Casenote Law Outline on Book, Chapter 1, § I.]

ENCYCLOPEDIA BRITANNICA v. COMMISSIONER
Publisher (P) v. IRS (D)
685 F.2d 212 (7th Cir. 1982).

NATURE OF CASE: Appeal from Tax Court decision allowing a business expense deduction.

FACT SUMMARY: The IRS (D) contended that an expenditure by Encyclopedia Britannica (P) for a manuscript which it planned to publish was a capital expenditure and, therefore, not currently deductible.

CONCISE RULE OF LAW: Where an expenditure is made with the intent that it will generate income over a period of years, it is classified as a capital expenditure and is not currently deductible as a business expense.

FACTS: Encyclopedia Britannica (P) hired David-Stewart Publishing to produce a manuscript for a book to be published by Encyclopedia Britannica (P). Normally they produced manuscripts in-house, but due to a shortage of employees they were forced to go outside. David-Stewart was to turn over a complete manuscript according to Britannica's (P) specifications, and it was to work closely with Britannica's (P) editorial department. In exchange, David-Stewart received advances against expected royalties. Britannica (P) treated the advances as ordinary and necessary business expenses deductible in the year in which they were paid. The IRS (D) contended they were capital expenditures and disallowed the deductions. Britannica (P) sought a redetermination of the assessed deficiency and the Tax Court held the expenditures were in return for services, rather than an asset, and concluded they were currently deductible. The IRS (D) appealed, contending that because the expenditures were made intending to realize income over a period of years, they were capital contributions.

ISSUE: Is an expenditure a capital contribution if it is made with the intent to generate income over a period of years?

HOLDING AND DECISION: (Posner, J.) Yes. Where an expenditure is made with the intent to generate income over a period of years, it is considered a capital expenditure deductible over the useful life of the asset purchased, rather than immediately deductible in the year in which they were made. The purchase of the manuscript is analogous to the purchase of any rental property, and the expenditures made to produce rental property are clearly capital expenditures. Britannica (P) expected to generate income from the manuscript beyond the year of the expenditures. Further, they were not expenditures ordinarily made by Britannica (P) who would ordinarily have produced the manuscript in-house. As a result, the advances were capital expenditures and not currently deductible as a business expense. Reversed.

EDITOR'S ANALYSIS: The court, in dicta, recognized that in some cases, there is a practical reason for authors and publishers to deduct their expenses immediately. They are in the business of producing a series of assets that will generate income over time. It is necessary for proper capitalization to identify particular expenditures with particular books because each book has a different useful life. Because of the difficulty in matching expenditures to individual books, which tend to be jointly made among several books, current deductibility would be more workable.

[For more information on capital expenditures, see Casenote Law Outline on Federal Income Taxation, Chapter 6, § I, Distinguishing Capital Expenditures from Expenses.]

QUICKNOTES

BUSINESS EXPENSE - A cost incurred or amounts expended as "ordinary and necessary expenses" in the process of conducting an income-generating activity, currently deductible from a taxpayer's liability.

CAPITAL EXPENDITURE - Expenditure which is not deductible currently (because it does not produce a decrease in wealth) but which creates, or adds to, basis.

NOTES:

MIDLAND EMPIRE PACKING CO. v. COMMISSIONER
Corporation (P) v. IRS (P)
14 T.C. 635 (1950).

NATURE OF CASE: Appeal from Commissioner's (D) decision holding that the oil proofing of a basement was a capital improvement.

FACT SUMMARY: Midland Empire Packing (P) oil proofed its basement to protect against oil seepage from a nearby refinery.

CONCISE RULE OF LAW: A structural change which does not increase the useful life or use of a building and which is the normal method of dealing with a given problem is a "repair" for tax purposes.

FACTS: Midland Empire Packing (P) used its basement for curing hides. After using it for this purpose for 25 years, Midland (P) discovered that oil seepage was occurring from a nearby refinery. The basement was oil-proofed and Midland (P) attempted to deduct the oil proofing as an ordinary and necessary business expense. The Commissioner (D) denied the deduction claiming that it was a capital improvement and should be depreciated.

ISSUE: Should a structural change which does not add to the life or use of a building, and is the normal manner of dealing with a specific situation, be capitalized?

HOLDING AND DECISION: (Arundell, J.) No. A repair merely serves to keep property in an operating condition over the probable life of the property and for the purpose for which it was used. It adds nothing of value to the property, merely maintains it. Section 162 permits deductions for ordinary and necessary business expenses. While the Commissioner (D) concedes that the oil proofing was necessary, he claimed that it was not an ordinary expense. Ordinary does not mean that an expense must be habitual. It merely requires that, based on experience, the expense would be a common and accepted means of combating a given problem. Here, neither the life or use of the basement was changed. Certainly, oil proofing is the normal means of combating oil seepage. The fact that the problem did not exist for 25 years is not determinative. Once it occurred, Midland (P) dealt with it in a normal and acceptable manner. The oil proofing was a repair rather than a capital improvement. The Commissioner's (D) decision is overturned.

EDITOR'S ANALYSIS: Hotel Sulgrave, Inc. v. Commissioner, 21 T.C. 619 (1954), held that the addition of a sprinkler system, even though ordered by the state, was a capital improvement. The court held that while it did not extend the use or life of the hotel, it made the property more valuable for use in petitioner's business through its compliance with state requirements.

[For more information on capital improvements, see Casenote Law Outline on Federal Income Taxation, Chapter 6, § I, Distinguishing Capital Expenditures from Expenses.]

QUICKNOTES

DEPRECIATION - An amount given to a taxpayer as an offset to gross income, to account for the reduction in value of the taxpayer's income producing property due to everyday usage.

NOTES:

NORWEST CORP. AND SUBSIDIARIES v. COMMISSIONER

Builder/remodeler (P) v. Commissioner (D)

T.C., 108 T.C. 265 (1997).

NATURE OF CASE: Determination of deductibility of business expenses.

FACT SUMMARY: Norwest Corp. (P) sought to deduct expenses associated with the removal of asbestos from its building in association with a remodeling project.

CONCISE RULE OF LAW: Where a taxpayer incurs costs associated with the improvement of property so that the value of the property is increased, its use is prolonged, or it is fashioned for a different use, such expense is classified as a capital improvement and must be capitalized.

FACTS: Norwest Corp. (P) constructed a building with asbestos-containing fireproofing materials, then decided to remove the fireproofing as part of a remodeling project. Norwest (P) subsequently attemped to deduct the costs of removing the asbestos-containing materials as ordinary and necessary business expenses. The Commissioner (D) disallowed the deductions because the removal was neither incidental nor a repair.

ISSUE: Where a taxpayer incurs costs associated with the improvement of property so that the value of the property is increased, its use prolonged, or it is fashioned for a different use, is such expense properly classified as a capital improvement?

HOLDING AND DECISION: [Judge not named.] Yes. Where a taxpayer incurs costs associated with the improvement of property so that the value of the property is increased, its use is prolonged, or it is fashioned for a different use, such expense is classified as a capital improvement and must be capitalized. In contrast, a repair is defined as an ordinary and necessary expense needed to keep the property in effective functioning condition. Repairs are deductible. The burden is on the taxpayer to demonstrate his entitlement to the proposed deduction. The deductibility of an expense is a question of fact for the court, which must examine the attendant facts and circumstances of the particular case. Generally, where a taxpayer undertakes an overall plan to rehabilitate or improve his property, such expenditures made in relation thereto must be capitalized. Additionally, where such a plan also encompasses necessary and ordinary expenses that would be deductible independently, such expenses must be capitalized as well. Here Norwest Corp. (P) removed the asbestos from its building pursuant to a general rehabilitation program. The decision to remove the asbestos was made after the remodeling program had already been approved and commenced. The removal of the asbestos was necessary in order to properly execute the remodeling work and to avoid later additional expense. Furthermore, had it not been for the commencement of the remodeling program, the presence of the asbestos would never have been detected. Thus, the costs incurred in removing the asbestos are not deductible and must be capitalized.

EDITOR'S ANALYSIS: The distinction between a capital expenditure and an expense made in relation to a particular asset determines whether the expenditure must be added to the basis of the property, or is properly deductible in the year in which it is incurred. Such expenditures are labeled as either "improvements" or "repairs." The Tax Code defines an improvement as an expenditure made in relation to existing property that either changes its purpose, prolongs its utility, or enhances its worth.

[For more information on capital expenditures, see Casenote Law Outline on Federal Income Taxation, Chapter 6, § I, Distinguishing Capital Expenditures from Expenses.]

QUICKNOTES

CAPITAL EXPENDITURE - Expenditure which is not deductible currently (because it does not produce a decrease in wealth) but which creates, or adds to, basis.

CAPITALIZED EXPENSE - An cost expended during an event or occurrence significant for tax purposes, assigned to long term value based on continuing expenses incurred or expected in the future.

COST - An amount that is considered the equivalent in value for an item of goods or an activity or event.

DEDUCTION - Subtraction (from gross income) in arriving at taxable income (the tax base).

NOTES:

STARR'S ESTATE v. COMMISSIONER
Decedent's estate (P) v. Commissioner (D)
274 F.2d 294 (9th Cir. 1959).

NATURE OF CASE: Action for a tax refund.

FACT SUMMARY: Starr (P), a business owner, had a sprinkler system installed under a lease agreement which provided for annual payments for five years of $1,240 and an option to renew for another five years at the annual rate of $32. Starr (P) claimed an ordinary business deduction for the annual rent, but the Commissioner (D) disallowed this, stating that the contract was in actuality a sale, thus the sprinkler must be capitalized.

CONCISE RULE OF LAW: A rental contract in which property is transferred that provides for a nominal price for renewal at termination will be treated as a contract of sale.

FACTS: Starr (P) had a sprinkler system installed at his place of business. The sprinkler was leased to Starr (P) for five years at the annual rate of $1,240. Starr (P) was given the option of renewing the lease for an additional five years for the annual rate of $32. The Commissioner (D) determined that the lease was in actuality a sale, therefore, the annual payments were not deductible as rent, but were capital expenditures that must be depreciated. The Tax Court sustained the Commissioner (D).

ISSUE: Is a rental agreement in which property is transferred that provides for a nominal price for renewal at termination to be treated for tax purposes as a contract of sale?

HOLDING AND DECISION: (Chambers, J.) Yes. When a transfer of property has occurred and at the end of the contract only a nominal price is required for renewal, then such an agreement for tax purposes will be treated as a sale of property. In this case, the bare facts support this conclusion. The sprinkler system was tailor-made for this particular piece of property. If there would be removal of the system, then the salvage value would be negligible. It stretches the imagination to believe that the lessor would ever intend to reclaim the system. Finally, it is obvious that the nominal rental payments after the five years were just a service charge for inspection. We conclude that the contract was a sale of property, therefore, the annual payments were a capital expenditure that must be depreciated in order to acquire a deduction. Affirmed.

EDITOR'S ANALYSIS: The student should note that the treatment by the tax court on whether a transaction is a sale or lease is similar to the way courts treat the same transaction to determine whether filing under Article 9 of the Uniform Commercial Code is required in order to perfect a security interest. If the transaction is a lease, no filing is required, whereas, if it is a sale then a filing is required. The courts use the rule of thumb test. If the option price amounts to 25 percent or more of the total list price, then the transaction is a lease; if it is less than 25 percent, then it is a sale.

[For more information on capital expenditures, see Casenote Law Outline on Federal Income Taxation, Chapter 6, § I, Distinguishing Capital Expenditures from Expenses.]

QUICKNOTES

AMORTIZED INTEREST - Additional amounts paid to reflect the further cost incurred by a lender, paid gradually over time in amounts that, when aggregated, will be sufficient to discharge the debt.

LEASE - An agreement or contract which creates a relationship between a landlord and tenant (real property) or lessor and lessee (real or personal property).

SALE OR EXCHANGE - An exchange of property for value in a transaction involving equal amounts exchanged, in contrast to property disposed of by gift or devise.

NOTES:

WELCH v. HELVERING
Debt repayer (P) v. Commissioner (D)
290 U.S. 111 (1933).

NATURE OF CASE: Appeal from decision of court of appeals affirming Commissioner's (D) determination that repayment of bankrupt corporation's debts were capital expenditures.

FACT SUMMARY: A grain commission agent, Welch (P), repaid debts of the bankrupt corporation he used to work for.

CONCISE RULE OF LAW: In order to be deductible, an expense must be "ordinary" in the business area practiced by the taxpayer.

FACTS: Welch (P) felt that it would be to his advantage to repay the debts owed by a bankrupt company that he used to work for. Therefore, over a period of years he took a percentage of his income and repaid these discharged debts. Welch (P) attempted to deduct these payments from his income as ordinary and necessary business expenses. The Commissioner (D) disallowed them claiming that they were capital expenditures for reputation and goodwill. The Tax Court and court of appeals sustained the Commissioner (D).

ISSUE: May extraordinary expenditures be deducted from income as business expenses?

HOLDING AND DECISION: (Cardozo, J.) No. The repayment of these debts may have been helpful or even necessary for the development of Welch's (P) business. At least Welch (P) thought that they were important. However, in order to qualify as a deduction, the expense must also be "ordinary." While it is difficult to define, "ordinary" means that it would be accepted practice in a given segment of the business world. The mere fact that an individual conceives of a moral duty or necessity for a given expense is not determinative. It must be the normal method, based on experience, for dealing with a given situation. Since Welch's (P) actions of repaying the debts of a bankrupt company are extraordinary, to say the least, they do not qualify as an ordinary and necessary business expense. The decision of the Commissioner (D) is sustained.

EDITOR'S ANALYSIS: For an example of a decision upholding a similar taxpayer claim see Dunn and McCarthy, Inc. v. Commissioner, 139 F.2d 242 (2d Cir. 1943). In that case, a corporation repaid certain employees who had lent money to the corporation's former president. The corporation was allowed the deductions on the grounds that they were made to promote and protect the taxpayer's existing business. The court held that the payments were not extraordinary and other corporations might well act in a similar manner. Welch was distinguished because it involved a new business.

[For more information on nondeductible outlays, see Casenote Law Outline on Federal Income Taxation, Chapter 7, § I, Expenses Relating to the Production of Income as Opposed to Those Relating to Personal Consumption.]

QUICKNOTES
BUSINESS EXPENSE - A cost incurred or amounts expended as "ordinary and necessary expenses" in the process of conducting an income-generating activity, currently deductible from a taxpayer's liability.

CAPITAL EXPENDITURE - Expenditure which is not deductible currently (because it does not produce a decrease in wealth) but which creates, or adds to, basis.

DEBT - An obligation incurred by a person who promises to render payment or compensation to another.

DEDUCTION - Subtraction (from gross income) in arriving at taxable income (the tax base).

NOTES:

GILLIAM v. COMMISSIONER

Artist (P) v. IRS (D)

51 T.C.M. 515 (1986).

NATURE OF CASE: Petition seeking to validate deduction of legal expenses and settlement funds.

FACT SUMMARY: Gilliam (P) petitioned the Tax Court seeking a determination that certain legal expenses incurred in defense of incidents occurring during a business plane trip were deductible as ordinary expenses of Gilliam's (P) trade or business.

CONCISE RULE OF LAW: Where activities giving rise to a taxpayer's legal expenses were not activities directly in the conduct of the taxpayer's trade or business, the expenses are not deductible as an ordinary and necessary business expense.

FACTS: Gilliam (P) was a well-known artist who also occasionally lectured and taught art. He also had a history of mental and emotional disturbances and was under continuous psychiatric and medical care. He accepted an invitation to teach and lecture for a week in Memphis. The evening before, feeling anxious about the trip, he obtained a prescription for the drug Dalmane. After leaving on the trip to Memphis, and while taking Dalmane, he became extremely nervous and anxious, threatened crew members, and assaulted a passenger. At the end of the flight, he was arrested and indicted on a number of criminal charges and settled the civil action. Gilliam (P) sought to deduct the legal expenses and the amount paid in settlement as ordinary expenses incurred in the course of his business. The Commissioner (D) disallowed the deduction, and from this decision, Gilliam (P) petitioned for review.

ISSUE: Where activities giving rise to the taxpayer's legal expenses were not activities directly in the conduct of the taxpayer's business or trade, are the expenses deductible as an ordinary and necessary business expense?

HOLDING AND DECISION: No. Where activities giving rise to a taxpayer's legal expenses were not activities directly in the conduct of the taxpayer's trade or business, the expenses are not deductible as an ordinary and necessary business expense. The incidents on the plane can hardly be characterized as events in the ordinary course of Gilliam's (P) trade or business. These incidents hardly occur frequently or ordinarily in the course of an artist's career. While it may be ordinary to travel in the course of an artist's business, altercations leading to criminal charges are another matter. Altercations such as this can occur in the course of transportation connected with Gilliam's (P) trade or business, but not directly in the course of the trade or business. The expenses are not deductible. Sustained.

EDITOR'S ANALYSIS: Situations like this might, on deeper analysis, give rise to causation problems. The court may have assumed that Gilliam's (P) profession had little to do with the incident. One could assume, however, that the pressures of the artist's profession brought about the anxiety felt by Gilliam (P) and the subsequent incident.

[For more information on legal expenses, see Casenote Law Outline on Federal Income Taxation, Chapter 7, § I, Expenses Relating to the Production of Income as Opposed to Those Relating to Personal Consumption.]

NOTES:

STEPHENS v. COMMISSIONER
Taxpayer (P) v. IRS (D)
905 F.2d 667 (2d Cir. 1990).

NATURE OF CASE: Appeal from denial of tax deduction.

FACT SUMMARY: In Stephens' (P) action against the Commissioner (D), challenging the Commissioner's (D) decision to disallow him a deduction for a restitution payment he was ordered to pay in satisfaction of fraud conviction, the tax court agreed with the Commissioner (D).

CONCISE RULE OF LAW: A deduction may not be allowed for uncompensated losses sustained during the taxable year when it would frustrate public policy.

FACTS: After Stephens (P) was convicted for defrauding Raytheon out of $530,000, he was ordered, as part of his sentencing, to make restitution to Raytheon for, in relevant part, this amount. Pursuant to this order, Stephens (P) made the restitution but was disallowed by the Commissioner (D) to claim it as a deduction. Accordingly, he brought suit against the Commissioner (D) in Tax Court, unsuccessfully challenging the Commissioner's (D) decision. Stephens (P) appealed.

ISSUE: May a deduction be allowed for uncompensated losses sustained during the taxable year when it would frustrate public policy?

HOLDING AND DECISION: No. A deduction may not be allowed for uncompensated losses sustained during the taxable year when it would frustrate public policy. This rule merely restates the common law principle as augmented by § 165 of the Tax Code, the latter of which allows deductions for uncompensated losses sustained during the taxable year. The above rule, then, represents a public policy exception to § 165's mandate. Moreover, this exception has been codified, to a qualified extent, in § 162 of the Code. Section 162's exception, in relevant part, disallows deduction for fines or similar penalties paid to a government for the violation of any law. Nevertheless, although Congress did not explicitly amend § 165 to embody § 162-like exceptions, the public policy considerations relevant to § 162 are also relevant to § 165. In the instant case, since Stephens' (P) restitution payment would not frustrate public policy, does not constitute a fine or similar penalty, or was not paid to a government, nothing bars his entitlement to a deduction. Reversed and remanded.

EDITOR'S ANALYSIS: In Tank Truck Rentals, Inc. v. Commissioner, the court articulated the common law test of nondeductibility that excepts § 165's mandate by noting, in effect, that where a deduction would "severely and immediately" frustrate public policy, it is disallowed. However, given the Stephens' court's observation that Congress has not codified this exception to § 165, it is obvious that a court has wide discretion to determine which deductions pass muster under the above test.

[For more information on deductions for business expenses, see Casenote Law Outline on Federal Income Taxation, Chapter 7, § I, Expenses Relating to the Production of Income.]

QUICKNOTES
RESTITUTION - The return or restoration of what the defendant has gained in a transaction to prevent the unjust enrichment of the defendant.

NOTES:

KNETSCH v. UNITED STATES
Taxpayer (D) v. Federal government (P)
364 U.S. 361 (1960).

NATURE OF CASE: Appeal of disallowance of deduction.

FACT SUMMARY: Knetsch (D) purchased an annuity under a contract by which he was to pay 32 percent interest, but he annually received back the cash value of the annuity.

CONCISE RULE OF LAW: I.R.C. § 163 permits taxpayers to deduct all "interest paid. . . on indebtedness," but, where a taxpayer enters into a sham loan transaction which serves no purpose except to reduce the amount of that taxpayer's tax, such deduction will not be allowed.

FACTS: Knetsch (D) purchased ten $400,000 deferred bonds from the Sam Houston Life Insurance Company for $4,000 cash and $4 million in 3½ percent interest annuity loan notes. As part of the purchase contract, Knetsch (D) was permitted to borrow any excess of the cash value of the bonds over his indebtedness before it was due annually. In 1954, he paid the first year's interest of $140,000 to the insurance company, then he borrowed what was to be the increase in value over that year, $99,000, and paid $3,465 interest on that. At year end, Knetsch (D) attempted to deduct $143,465 from his income tax return under I.R.C. § 163. He repeated this process for two more years before he terminated the contract. From a disallowance of his deductions, this appeal followed.

ISSUE: May a taxpayer enter a loan transaction with the sole purpose of avoiding income taxes under I.R.C. § 163?

HOLDING AND DECISION: (Brennan, J.) No. I.R.C. § 163 permits taxpayers to deduct all "interest paid . . . on indebtedness," but, where a taxpayer enters into a sham loan transaction which serves no purpose except to reduce the amount of that taxpayer's tax, such deduction will not be allowed. It is true that "the legal right of a taxpayer to decrease . . . his taxes, or altogether avoid them . . . cannot be doubted," (Gregory v. Helvering) but this right can only be asserted in ways consistent with controlling I.R.C. sections. I.R.C. § 163 was drawn to give relief to taxpayers who have altered their economic condition by undertaking loans. No such alteration occurred here. Knetsch's (D) transaction with the insurance company had no affect on his economic position except to reduce his tax — no impact on his beneficial interest in his own funds occurred. This is a sham not included within I.R.C. § 163 provisions. The deduction was properly denied.

DISSENT: (Douglas, J.) Justice Douglas would permit the deduction. Tax avoidance is a business reality. Absent specific I.R.C. provisions outlawing the plan employed here, the Court should not seek to deny its deductions through "interpretations" of the tax code.

EDITOR'S ANALYSIS: I.R.C. § 163 permits every taxpayer — not just businessmen — to deduct all interest paid or accrued on indebtedness. The indebtedness must be that of the taxpayer personally — the taxpayer must be responsible for the indebtedness. The taxpayer need not necessarily be personally "liable," however. A deduction will not be denied merely because the creditor involved may look to some collateral (even if put up by a third party) for repayment. Note also that any indebtedness incurred, even if not a sham, must have some significance independent of its tax consequences.

[For more information on deductibility of interest payments, see Casenote Law Outline on Federal Income Taxation, Chapter 7, § I, Expenses Relating to the Production of Income as Opposed to Those Relating to Personal Consumption.]

QUICKNOTES

ANNUITY - The payment or right to receive payment of a fixed sum periodically, for a specified time period.

NOTES:

ESTATE OF FRANKLIN v. COMMISSIONER

Decedent (P) v. IRS (D)

544 F.2d 1045 (9th Cir. 1976).

NATURE OF CASE: Appeal from an action seeking disallowance of a taxpayer's deductions.

FACT SUMMARY: Estate of Franklin (P) brought this action against the Tax Commissioner (D) after he sought to disallow deductions for Franklin's and six other doctors' distributive share of losses reported by a limited partnership with respect to its acquisition of a motel.

CONCISE RULE OF LAW: Depreciation is not predicated upon ownership of property but rather upon an investment in property.

FACTS: The Tax Commissioner (D) sought to disallow deductions for the distributive share of losses reported by Twenty-Fourth Property Associates (P), a California limited partnership of seven doctors of which decedent Franklin was one, with respect to its acquisition of a motel and related properties. These losses have their origin in deductions for depreciation and interest claimed with respect to these properties. Under a sales agreement, the owners of the Thunderbird Inn, an Arizona motel, agreed that the property would be paid for over a period of 10 years, with interest on any unpaid balance of 7½ percent per annum. Prepaid interest in the amount of $75,000 was payable immediately; monthly principal and interest installments of $9,045 would be paid for approximately the first 10 years, with Associates (P) required to make a balloon payment at the end of the 10 years, forecast as $975,000. The sale was combined with a leaseback of the property by Associates (P) and so they never took physical possession. The Tax Court, agreeing with the Commissioner (D), held that the transaction more nearly resembled an option than a sale, the benefits and burdens of ownership remaining with the original owners. Associates (P) appealed.

ISSUE: Is depreciation predicated upon ownership of property rather than upon an investment in property?

HOLDING AND DECISION: (Sneed, J.) No. An acquisition such as that of Associates (P) if at a price approximately equal to the fair market value of the property under ordinary circumstances would rather quickly yield an equity in the property which the purchaser could not prudently abandon. It meshes with the form of the transaction and constitutes a sale. No such meshing occurs when the purchase price exceeds a demonstrably reasonable estimate of the fair-market value. It is fundamental that depreciation is not predicated upon ownership of property but, rather, upon an investment in property. No such investment exists when payments of the purchase price in accordance with the design of the parties yield no equity to the purchaser. In the transaction before the court, the purchase price payments by Associates (P) have not been shown to constitute an investment in the property. Depreciation was properly disallowed. Only the original owners had an investment in the property. Affirmed.

EDITOR'S ANALYSIS: The court points out that its focus on the relationship of the fair-market value of the property to the unpaid purchase price should not be read as premised upon the belief that a sale is not a sale if the purchaser pays too much. Bad bargains from the buyer's point of view — as well as sensible bargains from buyer's, but exceptionally good from the seller's point of view — do not thereby cease to be sales. See Commissioner v. Brown, 380 U.S. 563 (1965); Union Bank v. United States, 285 F.2d 126 (1961). The holding was limited to transactions substantially similar to the one before the court.

[For more information on acquisition indebtedness, see Casenote Law Outline on Federal Income Taxation, Chapter 4, § I, Basis.]

QUICKNOTES

BASIS - The value assigned to a taxpayer's costs incurred as the result of acquiring an asset and used to compute tax amounts towards the transactions in which that asset is involved.

DEPRECIATION - An amount given to a taxpayer as an offset to gross income, to account for the reduction in value of the taxpayer's income producing property due to everyday usage.

NOTES:

PROSMAN v. COMMISSIONER
Taxpayer (D) v. IRS (P)
T.C. Memo 1999-87.

NATURE OF CASE: Tax deficiency action.

FACT SUMMARY: Prosman (D) challenged the applicability of the Alternative Minimum Tax.

CONCISE RULE OF LAW: The Alternative Minimum Tax is not inequitable.

FACTS: Prosman (D) worked as a computer consultant and requested that his employer pay a per diem allowance in addition to a standard pay rate. However, the employer refused and included all money as wages on Prosman's (D) W-2. Following Prosman's (D) reported income on his tax return, the IRS (P) determined that he was subject to the Alternative Minimum Tax (AMT) and determined a deficiency. Prosman (D) challenged the decision.

ISSUE: Is the Alternative Minimum Tax inequitable?

HOLDING AND DECISION: No. The Alternative Minimum Tax is not inequitable. Section 55(a) imposes a tax equal to the excess of the tentative minimum tax over the regular tax. In calculating AMT income, no deduction is allowed for miscellaneous itemized deductions and state and local taxes. Thus, in computing Prosman's (D) tax, deductions for taxes paid and job expenses were disallowed. Prosman's (D) contention that the AMT was intended to apply only to high income earners has no merit. Additionally, while the court sympathizes with Prosman (D) that he would not have been subject to the AMT if his employer had separated the per diem allowance, the tax code is clear that income must be treated as it was received. The IRS's (P) determination is sustained.

EDITOR'S ANALYSIS: In this case, Prosman (D) had only the argument that the AMT was unfair because the clear language of the law made him subject to it. Prosman had adjusted gross income of over $80,000 for the taxable year at issue. Many would consider him to be the type of high income earner that the tax was intended to cover.

QUICKNOTES
§55(a): Establishes an alternative minimum tax.

NOTES:

CHAPTER 7
THE SPLITTING OF INCOME

QUICK REFERENCE RULES OF LAW

1. **Income From Services: Diversion by Private Agreement.** A statute can tax salaries to those who earned them and can provide that a tax can not be escaped by anticipatory arrangements or contracts which prevent salary from vesting even for a second in the person who earned it. (Lucas v. Earl)

   [For more information on the "anticipatory assignment of income" doctrine, see Casenote Law Outline on Federal Income Taxation, Chapter 9, § III, Preventing Assignment of Income and Deductions.]

2. **Income From Services: Diversion by Operation of Law.** In a state in which the wife has a vested property right in the community property equal with that of her husband, and in the income of the community, each spouse may file a separate tax return treating one half of the community property as their separate income. (Poe v. Seaborn)

   [For more information on income from community property, see Casenote Law Outline on Federal Income Taxation, Chapter 9, § II, Attribution of Income and Deductions.]

3. **Income From Services: More on Diversion by Private Agreement.** Benefits received by employees in connection with their performance of services within the scope of their employment are compensatory in nature and must be included in their taxable income. (Armantrout v. Commissioner)

   [For more information on income from services, see Casenote Law Outline on Federal Income Taxation, Chapter 9, § II, Attribution of Income and Deductions.]

4. **Transfers of Property and Income from Property.** The beneficiary of a testamentary trust whose assignments of the income thereof are valid, is not taxable under the federal income tax act on the income so assigned. (Blair v. Commissioner)

   [For more information on income attribution doctrines, see Casenote Law Outline on Federal Income Taxation, Chapter 9, § III, Preventing Assignment of Income and Deductions.]

5. **Transfers of Property and Income from Property.** For income tax purposes the power to dispose of income is the equivalent of ownership of it, and the exercise of that power to transfer payment of the income to another is the equivalent of realization of the income. (Helvering v. Horst)

   [For more information on the power to control income, see Casenote Law Outline on Federal Income Taxation, Chapter 9, § III, Preventing Assignment of Income and Deductions.]

6. **Services Transformed into Property.** Renewal commissions assigned by the taxpayer are taxable to the taxpayer in the year in which they become payable. (Helvering v. Eubank)

   [For more information on income from services, see Casenote Law Outline on Federal Income Taxation, Chapter 9, § II, Attribution of Income and Deductions.]

7. **Services Transformed into Property.** When a patent right is transferred in exchange for royalty payments and the retained interest may be assigned without their being taxed to the assignor, in exchange for royalty payments and the taxpayer returns an interest in or control over it, the royalty payments and the retained interest may be assigned without their being taxed to the assignor. (Heim v. Fitzpatrick)

[For more information on "property" interests, see Casenote Law Outline on Federal Income Taxation, Chapter 9, § II, Attribution of Income and Deductions.]

8. **Gift and Leaseback.** The validity of a gift and leaseback transaction for tax purposes depends on: (1) the duration of the transfer; (2) the controls retained by the donor; (3) the use of the gift for the benefit of the donor; and (4) the independence of the trustee. (Brooke v. United States)

[For more information on the assignment of income doctrines, see Casenote Law Outline on Federal Income Taxation, Chapter 9, § III, Preventing Assignment of Income and Deductions.]

9. **Shifting Income through a Corporation.** Where a corporation is a viable, taxable entity and not a mere sham, the assignment of income doctrine does not apply to disregard the corporate form. (Foglesong v. Commissioner)

[For more information on assignment of income, see Casenote Law Outline on Book, Chapter 1, § I.]

10. **Pension Trust.** One cannot avoid taxation of one's earned income by entering into anticipatory assignments of the income. (United States v. Basye)

[For more information on pass-through entities, see Casenote Law Outline on Federal Income Taxation, Chapter 9, § I, Identity of Taxpayers.]

LUCAS v. EARL
Commissioner (D) v. Married joint tenants (P)
281 U.S. 111 (1930).

NATURE OF CASE: On writ of certiorari to review a decision of the Tax Court.

FACT SUMMARY: The Earls (D) entered into a contract whereby they agreed that whatever each acquired in any way during their marriage shall be received and owned by them as joint tenants. Hence, Mr. Earl (D) claims he can be taxed for only half of his income.

CONCISE RULE OF LAW: A statute can tax salaries to those who earned them and can provide that a tax can not be escaped by anticipatory arrangements or contracts which prevent salary from vesting even for a second in the person who earned it.

FACTS: The Earls (D) entered into a contract whereby they agreed that whatever each acquired in any way during their marriage shall be received and owned by them as joint tenants. Mr. Earl (D) claims that due to the contract he can only be taxed for one half of his income for 1920 and 1921. The validity of the contract is not questioned.

ISSUE: Can an anticipatory contract prevent a salary from vesting, for tax purposes, in the person who earned it?

HOLDING AND DECISION: (Holmes, J.) No. Section 213(a) imposes a tax upon the net income of every individual including income derived from salaries, wages, or compensation for personal service of whatever kind and in whatever form paid. There is no doubt that the statute could tax salaries as to those who earned them. The tax could not be escaped by anticipatory arrangements and contracts however skillfully devised to prevent the salary from vesting even for a second in the person who earned it. This is true whatever the motives for the contract might have been.

EDITOR'S ANALYSIS: The Earls lived in California. Under that state's community property laws the wife did not have a vested interest in the husband's earnings until 1927. In Commissioner v. Harmon, 323 U.S. 44, the court held a 1939 Oklahoma statute permitting spouses to elect to be governed by a community property system was not effective for federal income taxation. The Court said that the existence of an option resulted in a status similar to that in Lucas v. Earl and distinguished Poe v. Seaborn, where "the court was not dealing with a consensual community, but one made an incident of marriage by the inveterate policy of the state." The dissent argued that Lucas v. Earl and Poe v. Seaborn state competing theories of income tax liability.

[For more information on the "anticipatory assignment of income" doctrine, see Casenote Law Outline on Federal Income Taxation, Chapter 9, § III, Preventing Assignment of Income and Deductions.]

QUICKNOTES

COMMUNITY PROPERTY - Property owned jointly by both spouses during a marriage, and which both spouses have equal rights of control over.

GROSS INCOME - The total income earned by an individual or business.

JOINT TENANCY - An interest in property whereby a single interest is owned by two or more persons and created by a single instrument; joint tenants possess equal interests in the use of the entire property and the last survivor is entitled to absolute ownership.

NET INCOME - The income of a business determined by subtracting costs and taxes from the total income.

NOTES:

POE v. SEABORN
IRS (P) v. Taxpayer (D)
282 U.S. 101 (1930).

NATURE OF CASE: On writ of certiorari to review a Tax Court decision.

FACT SUMMARY: The Seaborns (D) filed separate tax returns, each treating one half of the community income as their separate incomes, although most of it consisted of Mr. Seaborn's (D) salary.

CONCISE RULE OF LAW: In a state in which the wife has a vested property right in the community property equal with that of her husband, and in the income of the community, each spouse may file a separate tax return treating one half of the community property as their separate income.

FACTS: The Seaborn's (D) income consisted of Mr. Seaborn's (D) salary, interests on bank deposits, dividends, and profits on sales of real property. The Seaborns (D) filed separate tax returns, each treating one half of the community income as their separate incomes. The Commissioner claimed that all of the income should have been reported on Mr. Seaborn's (D) return. The Seaborns (D) lived in Washington, which was a community property state in which the wife could borrow for community purposes and bind the community property, sue her husband to enjoin collection of his debts out of the property, and prevent his making gifts out of the property.

ISSUE: In a state in which the wife has a vested right in the community property, may each spouse file a separate tax return treating one half of the community property as their separate income?

HOLDING AND DECISION: (Roberts, J.) Yes. In a state in which the wife has a vested property right in the community property, equal with that of her husband, and in the community income, each spouse may file a separate tax return treating one half of the community property as their separate income. In Washington, where the Seaborn's (D) lived, while the husband has the management and control of the community property, this power is subject to restrictions which are inconsistent with denial of the wife's interest as co-owner. It is clear that under Washington law a wife has a vested property right in the community property, and, hence, may file a return treating one half of such property as her separate income.

EDITOR'S ANALYSIS: In common law property states, if the husband makes an outright gift to his wife of property, the income subsequently produced by the property is taxed to her. If he transfers the property into a joint tenancy or a tenancy in common with his wife, the income will be divided between them for tax purposes. But ordinarily, the common law couple cannot split up the husband's earned income for tax purposes, and splitting of investment income will be jeopardized if the husband retains control over either the transferred property or the income.

[For more information on income from community property, see Casenote Law Outline on Federal Income Taxation, Chapter 9, § II, Attribution of Income and Deductions.]

NOTES:

ARMANTROUT v. COMMISSIONER
Employee (P) v. IRS (D)
67 T.C. 996 (1977); aff'd, 570 F.2d 210 (7th Cir. 1978).

NATURE OF CASE: Appeal from deficiency assessment.

FACT SUMMARY: The IRS (D) contended that amounts distributed according to an education scholarship plan were includable in the employee recipient's taxable income as a form of deferred compensation.

CONCISE RULE OF LAW: Benefits received by employees in connection with their performance of services within the scope of their employment are compensatory in nature and must be included in their taxable income.

FACTS: Hamlin contracted with Educo, a company that designed, implemented, and administered college education benefit plans for employers, to supply such a plan to key employees. The plan allocated a certain amount as scholarships to offset the cost of a college education. Only key employees were eligible to participate, and the plan was used as a work incentive and as a tool in recruitment. If an employee left Hamlin's employ, he became ineligible. The use of the plan succeeded in retaining key employees and attracting qualified applicants without Hamlin having to raise salaries to stay competitive. Armantrout (P) was an employee whose children received benefits under the plan. The IRS (D) assessed a deficiency against him, contending the amounts received were forms of compensation and includable in his taxable income. Armantrout (P) petitioned the Tax Court for a redetermination.

ISSUE: Are benefits received in connection with an employee's performance of services compensatory in nature and therefore, taxable income?

HOLDING AND DECISION: Yes. Benefits received by employees in connection with the performance of services within their employment are compensatory in nature. Armantrout (P) was eligible for the plan based solely on his value to the company. This value was directly related to the quality of service he performed within his employment. Further, the fact that upon leaving Hamlin's employ, Armantrout (P) would become ineligible strengthens the conclusion that the amounts received under the plan were tied to employment and, therefore, were compensatory in nature. Therefore, they must be included in income. Judgment for the IRS (D).

EDITOR'S ANALYSIS: Although the IRS (D) in this case did not raise § 83(a) of the Internal Revenue Code, that section clearly supports the holding in this case. It states in effect that as a general rule, where property is given to one person in consideration of the performance of services by another, the value of the property must be included in the taxable income of the party performing the services.

[For more information on income from services, see Casenote Law Outline on Federal Income Taxation, Chapter 9, § II, Attribution of Income and Deductions.]

QUICKNOTES

DEFERRED COMPENSATION - Earnings that are to be taxed at the time that they are received by, or distributed to, the employee and not when they are in fact earned.

NOTES:

BLAIR v. COMMISSIONER

Trust beneficiary (D) v. Commissioner (P)
300 U.S. 5 (1937).

NATURE OF CASE: On certiorari to review a reversal of a Tax Court decision.

FACT SUMMARY: Blair (D), the beneficiary of a testamentary trust, assigned interests in the trusts to his children. The trustees distributed the income from such interests directly to the children.

CONCISE RULE OF LAW: The beneficiary of a testamentary trust whose assignments of the income are valid, will not be taxed on the income so assigned.

FACTS: The will of Blair's (D) father created a trust and called for payment of all income to Blair (D) during his life. Blair (D) assigned interests in the trust to his children. The trustees accepted the assignments and distributed the income directly to the assignees. The Court found the assignments to be valid.

ISSUE: Is a beneficiary of a testamentary trust liable for a tax upon income from the trust which he had assigned to his children?

HOLDING AND DECISION: (Hughes, J.) No. The tax here is not upon earnings which are taxed to the one who earns them, nor is it a case of income attributable to a taxpayer by reason of the application of the income to the discharge of his obligation. There is no question of evasion or of Blair's (D) retention of control here. If under the law governing the trust, the beneficial interest is assignable, and if it has been assigned without reservation, the assignee thus becomes the beneficiary and is entitled to rights and remedies accordingly, hence the beneficiary of a testamentary trust whose assignments of the income thereof are valid is not taxable under the federal income tax act on the income so assigned. Blair (D) is not liable for the income which he assigned to his children.

EDITOR'S ANALYSIS: Some transfers are ineffective to redirect income from the donor for federal income purposes. A father who tries to assign in advance a portion of his paycheck to his child will nevertheless be treated as the recipient of income (Lucas v. Earl). On the other hand, if a woman gives Blackacre to her daughter in fee, it is, of course, appropriate to tax the income from Blackacre to the daughter. There are innumerable gradations between these two extremes, and it is very difficult to draw a consistent boundary.

[For more information on income attribution doctrines, see Casenote Law Outline on Federal Income Taxation, Chapter 9, § III, Preventing Assignment of Income and Deductions.]

HELVERING v. HORST
Commissioner (P) v. Bond owner (D)
311 U.S. 112 (1940).

NATURE OF CASE: On writ of certiorari to review a reversal of a Tax Court decision.

FACT SUMMARY: Shortly before their due date, Horst (D) detached negotiable interest coupons from negotiable bonds and gave them to his son who in the same year collected them at maturity.

CONCISE RULE OF LAW: For income tax purposes the power to dispose of income is the equivalent of ownership of it, and the exercise of that power to transfer payment of the income to another is the equivalent of realization of the income.

FACTS: Horst (D) owned some negotiable bonds from which he detached the negotiable interest coupons shortly before their due date and gave them to his son. The son, in the same year, collected them at maturity. The Commissioner claimed that the interest payments were taxable to Horst (D).

ISSUE: Will a donor be taxed for interest payments on negotiable interest coupons which he detached, shortly before they were due, from negotiable bonds and gave to a donee who collected them at maturity in the same year?

HOLDING AND DECISION: (Stone, J.) Yes. The power to dispose of income is the equivalent of ownership of it. The exercise of that power to procure the payment of income to another is the enjoyment and, hence, the realization of the income by he who exercises it. The owner of negotiable bonds stands in the place of the lender. When by the gift of the coupons he separates his right to interest payments, as Horst (D) did here, and procured the payment of the interest to the donee, he has enjoyed the economic benefits of the income in the same manner and to the same extent as though the transfer were of earnings and in either case, the fruit is not to be attributed to a different tree from that on which it grew.

DISSENT: (McReynolds, J.) The coupons were independent negotiable instruments. Through the gift they became at once the absolute property of the son, free from Horst's (D) control and should not be taxable to him.

EDITOR'S ANALYSIS: If the doctrine of Horst were applied literally, a donor who gave Blackacre in 1930 might still be taxable on the income from it in 1960. On the other hand, the doctrine of Blair, that where ownership of property is transferred the income arising therefrom cannot be taxed to the donor, has been criticized as restricting taxation of the donor too narrowly, since every inchoate right to past or future income may be said to be "property." In Horst, the court distinguished Blair on the nature of the gift and the income transferred, frequently a determining issue.

[For more information on the power to control income, see Casenote Law Outline on Federal Income Taxation, Chapter 9, § III, Preventing Assignment of Income and Deductions.]

QUICKNOTES
GROSS INCOME - The total income earned by an individual or business.

NEGOTIABLE INSTRUMENT - A signed writing promising to pay a specific sum of money either on demand or at a specified time.

NOTES:

HELVERING v. EUBANK
IRS (D) v. Life insurance agent (P)
311 U.S. 122 (1940).

NATURE OF CASE: Appeal from decision finding commissions taxable income.

FACT SUMMARY: The Government (D) appealed from a decision upholding Eubank's (P) position that renewal commissions assigned by Eubank (P) were not taxable in the year in which they became payable.

CONCISE RULE OF LAW: Renewal commissions assigned by the taxpayer are taxable to the taxpayer in the year in which they become payable.

FACTS: Eubank (P) was a life insurance agent. After the termination of his agency contracts and services as an agent, he assigned renewal commissions to become payable for services rendered before his termination. The Commissioner (D) assessed the renewal commissions paid to the assignees as income to Eubank (P) in the year they became payable. Eubank (P) challenged this tax treatment, and from a decision holding that the commissions assigned by Eubank (P) were not taxable to him in the year they became payable, the Commissioner (D) appealed.

ISSUE: Are renewal commissions assigned by the taxpayer taxable to the taxpayer in the year they become payable?

HOLDING AND DECISION: (Stone, J.) Yes. Renewal commissions assigned by the taxpayer are taxable to the taxpayer in the year in which they become payable. Reversed.
SEPARATE OPINION: (McReynolds, J.) Upon assignment of the commissions, Eubank (P) could do nothing further with respect to them. In no sense were they earned or received by him during the taxable year. The court below was correct in stating that when a taxpayer who makes his income tax on a cash basis assigns a right to monies payable in the future for work already performed, he transfers a property right, and the money when paid is not taxable to the taxpayer in the year paid.

EDITOR'S ANALYSIS: Future commissions such as those involved in the present case involve an element of interest on the amount of the commission earned. Issues can arise to what amount to be taxed, whether it should be the present value of the commission assigned, or the face value of the amount of the commissions at the time of the assignment.

[For more information on income from services, see Casenote Law Outline on Federal Income Taxation, Chapter 9, § II, Attribution of Income and Deductions.]

QUICKNOTES

BASIS - The value assigned to a taxpayer's costs incurred as the result of acquiring an asset and used to compute tax amounts towards the transactions in which that asset is involved.

NOTES:

HEIM v. FITZPATRICK
Inventor (P) v. IRS (D)
262 F.2d 887 (2d Cir. 1959).

NATURE OF CASE: Appeal from Tax Court decision affirming Commissioner's (D) determination that the assignment of patent royalties was ineffective for tax purposes.

FACT SUMMARY: Heim (D) assigned his inventions in exchange for royalty payments. Heim (P) then assigned his royalty rights to his family.

CONCISE RULE OF LAW: When a patent right is transferred in exchange for royalty payments and the retained interest may be assigned without their being taxed to the assignor, in exchange for royalty payments and the taxpayer returns an interest in or control over it, the royalty payments and the retained interest may be assigned without their being taxed to the assignor.

FACTS: Heim (P) invented a new type of rod end and bearing. He transferred the invention to a company which was substantially owned by his wife and daughter in exchange for royalty payments. Heim (P) then transferred these payments, plus his retained interest and control over the patents, to his wife, son, and daughter. The Commissioner (D) determined that the transfer was ineffective and taxed the royalty payments to Heim (P). The Tax Court affirmed on the grounds that what was transferred was the right to receive income in exchange for past services, and also on the grounds that Heim (P) indirectly controlled the company through his wife's and daughter's stock holdings.

ISSUE: Where an interest in and control over a patent is retained, does the taxpayer possess a "property right" which will prevent royalty income from being allocated to him when it has been assigned to another?

HOLDING AND DECISION: (Swan, J.) Yes. Heim (P) retained an option to cancel the contract upon a specified contingency. Heim (P) also could negotiate price and restricted the transfer of the patent by the company. These are property rights which, when transferred with the royalty rights, were more than a mere right to receive future income. What Heim (P) gave to his family was, in effect, income-producing property. The Commissioner (D) further argues that Heim (P) had indirect control over the company and could control royalty payments. However, Heim (P) was neither an officer nor a major shareholder in the company. No evidence has been adduced that he could control the patent payments. The Tax Court's decision is overruled.

EDITOR'S ANALYSIS: Apparently the distinguishing factor in Heim and Strauss is the existence of a "property interest" in the transferror rather than a contractual right to profits from the property. Whether such interest exists seems to determine whether a case will be governed by Blair, in which case the income is not taxable to the transferror or by cases such as Strauss and Horst in which case the income is taxable to the transferror. Likewise, the related problem of whether the sale for consideration of certain income-producing rights gives rise to ordinary income or capital gains generally turns on whether the taxpayer sold "property" or "rights to income."

[For more information on "property" interests, see Casenote Law Outline on Federal Income Taxation, Chapter 9, § II, Attribution of Income and Deductions.]

NOTES:

BROOKE v. UNITED STATES
Physician (P) v. Federal government (D)
468 F.2d 1155 (9th Cir. 1972).

NATURE OF CASE: Appeal from grant of tax refund.

FACT SUMMARY: The IRS (D) contended that Brooke (P) had not transferred a sufficient property interest to support the validity of his transaction as a gift and leaseback.

CONCISE RULE OF LAW: The validity of a gift and leaseback transaction for tax purposes depends on: (1) the duration of the transfer; (2) the controls retained by the donor; (3) the use of the gift for the benefit of the donor; and (4) the independence of the trustee.

FACTS: Brooke (P), a physician, unconditionally deeded land to his children upon which was a pharmacy, a rental apartment, and the offices of his medical practice. Subsequently, he was appointed as guardian of the children, and in that capacity he collected rents from the apartment and the pharmacy. Also, without a written lease, he paid himself, as guardian, the reasonable rental value of his medical offices. He applied these rents to the children's insurance, health, and education expenses. The IRS (D) contended Brooke (P) failed to transfer a sufficient property interest in the land to support the validity of the transaction as a gift and leaseback. On this basis, it disallowed any business deductions in connection with the transfer. Brooke (P) successfully sued for a refund, and the IRS (D) appealed.

ISSUE: Does the validity of a gift and leaseback transaction depend on the duration of the transfer, the control retained by the donor, the use of the gift for the donor's benefit, and the independence of the trustee?

HOLDING AND DECISION: Yes. The validity of a gift and leaseback transaction for tax purposes depends on: (1) the duration of the transfer; (2) the controls retained by the donor; (3) the use of the gift for the benefit of the donor; and (4) the independence of the trustee. In this case, the transfer was unconditional, absolute, and irrevocable. Therefore, the durational element was met. Second, Brooke (P) retained no individual control over the property. All control was exercised as the children's guardian. He continued to pay rent and exercised only that control available to a tenant. Further, all rental payments were spent to benefit the children. Finally, as a court-appointed guardian, all dispositions of the property required court approval. As a court-appointed guardian, his trusteeship was sufficiently independent. As a result, the transaction was a valid gift and leaseback and the deductions were proper. Affirmed.

DISSENT: (Ely, J.) Because there was no identifiable business purpose to this transaction, it cannot be considered a valid gift and leaseback. The business purpose test is equally applicable to gift and leaseback situations as it is to sale and leaseback situations.

EDITOR'S ANALYSIS: Some commentators argue that a donor's status as a court-appointed guardian under court supervision does not afford the requisite level of independence to validate a gift and leaseback transaction. Under the Uniform Gifts to Minors Act, little if any court supervision is exercised, except in extreme cases wherein a custodian's actions are challenged.

[For more information on the assignment of income doctrines, see Casenote Law Outline on Federal Income Taxation, Chapter 9, § III, Preventing Assignment of Income and Deductions.]

NOTES:

FOGLESONG v. COMMISSIONER
Taxpayer (D) v. Internal Revenue Service (P)
621 F.2d 865 (7th Cir. 1980).

NATURE OF CASE: Appeal from tax court decision concluding commissions were taxable to the taxpayer and not a corporation.

FACT SUMMARY: The tax court determined that 98% of sales commissions earned by a personal service corporation established by Foglesong (D), a steel tubing sales representative, were taxable to Foglesong (D) and not the corporation.

CONCISE RULE OF LAW: Where a corporation is a viable, taxable entity and not a mere sham, the assignment of income doctrine does not apply to disregard the corporate form.

FACTS: Foglesong (D) incorporated his business in order to obtain limited liability production of the corporate structure and to provide a better vehicle for expansion into other business areas. The corporation paid him a regular salary as a salesman as well as paid all of his expenses, insurance coverage, maintained a company car, and complied with all corporate formalities of the state of New Jersey. The tax court concluded that, although there was no attempt by Foglesong (D) to take advantage of losses incurred by a separate business, the establishment of the corporation was motivated more by tax avoidance than genuine business concerns. The court concluded that 98% of the commission income remained with Foglesong (D) so that such income was taxable to him and not the corporation. With respect to those commissions that were earned solely because of the corporation's exclusive territorial rights, the court held that the commissions were properly taxable to the corporation. Foglesong (D) appealed.

ISSUE: Where a corporation is a viable, taxable entity and not a mere sham, does the assignment of income doctrine apply to disregard the corporate form?

HOLDING AND DECISION: (Cudahy, J.) No. Where a corporation is a viable, taxable entity and not a mere sham, the assignment of income doctrine does not apply to disregard the corporate form. The tax court did not decide the issue of whether the Commissioner (P) was permitted to allocate the commission income to Foglesong (D) under §482, which allows the reallocation of income and expenses among commonly controlled organizations, trades or businesses. The assignment of income doctrine under §61 seeks to attribute income, which is split artificially among several entities over different years, to the true earner by recognizing substance over form. Here the tax court found that the corporation was not a mere sham but a viable, taxable entity. Given these circumstances, it was inappropriate to weigh the business purposes as tax avoidance purposes in determining whether the assignment of income doctrine should apply to disregard the corporate form. In Rubin v. Commissioner, which involved similar facts, the tax court found the income was properly taxable to the individual and that the taxpayer controlled not only the personal service corporation but also the corporation to which the services were rendered. That decision is distinguishable in the present case. In a case where the issue is application of the assignment of income doctrine to effectively set aside the corporation such as here, an attempt to balance tax avoidance motives against legitimate business purposes is ineffective. Here §482 is available to allocate "gross income, deductions, credits or allowances" to prevent tax evasion or to show the actual taxpayer's income. The case is remanded to the tax court for consideration of the Commissioner's (P) §482 claims. Reversed and remanded.

DISSENT: (Wood, J.) While the tax court's view is preferable, §482 should apply.

EDITOR'S ANALYSIS: The tax court on remand, applying §482, reached the same conclusion. Foglesong (D) appealed and the court of appeals reversed and remanded again, stating that §482 was inapplicable and requesting a determination of whether the assignment of income doctrine was applicable "to allocate dividends and preferred stock received by Foglesong's (D) children to Foglesong" (D) himself. The tax court again concluded that the application of §482 is proper in cases involving personal service corporations established by a single individual.

QUICKNOTES
CORPORATION - A distinct legal entity characterized by continuous existence; free alienability of interests held therein; centralized management; and limited liability on the part of the shareholders of the corporation.

NOTES:

UNITED STATES v. BASYE
Federal government (P) v. Physicians (D)
410 U.S. 441 (1973).

NATURE OF CASE: Appeal from reversal of ruling that certain benefits be taxed as income.

FACT SUMMARY: A partnership of physicians did not report nor did the physician partners pay tax on amounts paid to a partnership retirement trust.

CONCISE RULE OF LAW: One cannot avoid taxation of one's earned income by entering into anticipatory assignments of the income.

FACTS: In 1959, the Permanente Medical Group, a partnership with over 200 physician-partners, entered into an agreement with the Kaiser Foundation Health Plan, Inc. to provide medical services to Kaiser's members in Northern California. As part of the compensation for these services, Kaiser agreed to pay retirement benefits to Permanente's partner and nonpartner physicians. A trust was established to which Kaiser made payments at a predetermined rate. The trust maintained a separate tentative account for each beneficiary. No beneficiary was eligible to receive payments from his tentative account prior to retirement; nor did the interest for each account vest prior to retirement. Kaiser paid over $2 million to the trust; however, Permanente did not report these payments as income in its partnership returns. Nor did the individual partners include these payments on the computations of their distributive shares of the partnership's taxable income. The Commissioner assessed deficiencies against each partner for his distributive share of the amount paid by Kaiser. The partners paid under protest and filed suit for refund. The district court of appeals reversed the Commissioner's decision. The United States (P) appealed.

ISSUE: Can taxation be avoided by entering into anticipatory assignments of one's income?

HOLDING AND DECISION: (Powell, J.) No. A partnership must report the income it generates and each partner must pay a portion of the total income as if the partnership were merely an agent or conduit through which the income passed. There is no question that Kaiser's payments to the partnership trust were compensation for services rendered by the partnership and thus should have been included as income in the partnership's returns. The fact that the payments were never actually received by the partnership but were paid directly to a trust is irrelevant. A basic rule of taxation is that an entity earning income — partnership or individual — cannot avoid taxation by entering into a contractual arrangement whereby that income is diverted to some other person or entity. Such anticipatory assignments of income have been held ineffective for over 40 years. The partnership's agreement with Kaiser for the payment of a portion of the

partnership's compensation to a trust fund is clearly an example of an anticipatory assignment of income: the partnership earned the income, and through a bargain with Kaiser had it diverted to a trust. Since the retirement payments should have been reported as income by the partnership, the individual partners should have declared their shares of that income on their individual returns. The fact that some of the partners, under the many conditions of the retirement agreement, might not ultimately receive anything is irrelevant. Once the income was received by the partnership the individual partners had to pay tax upon it. Reversed.

EDITOR'S ANALYSIS: Solicitor General Griswold argued this case himself, perhaps to indicate to the Supreme Court that it had some learning to do after its decision in Commissioner v. First Security Bank of Utah, 405 U.S. 394 (1972), which was seen as seriously undermining judicial precedents enforcing taxation against the person whose effort or capital produces an item of income.

[For more information on pass-through entities, see Casenote Law Outline on Federal Income Taxation, Chapter 9, § I, Identity of Taxpayers.]

QUICKNOTES

ASSIGNMENT - A transaction in which a party conveys his or her entire interest in property to another.

PARTNERSHIP - A voluntary agreement entered into by two or more parties to engage in business and to share any attendant profits and losses.

NOTES:

CHAPTER 8
CAPITAL GAINS AND LOSSES

QUICK REFERENCE RULES OF LAW

1. **Property Held "Primarily for Sale to Customers:" Sale to "Customers."** Taxpayers who buy securities for speculation or investment hold them as capital assets and not primarily for resale to customers. (Van Suetendael v. Commissioner)

   [For more information on capital assets, see Casenote Law Outline on Federal Income Taxation, Chapter 4, § V, Capital Gains and Losses.]

2. **Property Held "Primarily for Sale to Customers:" "Primarily for Sale."** When dispositions of subdivided property extend over a long period of time and are especially numerous, the likelihood that the profit on such dispositions is a capital gain is very slight. (Biedenharn Realty Co. v. United States)

   [For more information on capital gains, see Casenote Law Outline on Federal Income Taxation, Chapter 4, § V, Capital Gains and Losses.]

3. **Transactions Related to the Taxpayer.** Where the purchase of commodity futures is an integral part of a taxpayer's business, it is not a true capital investment, and gains or losses produce ordinary income or losses. (Corn Products Refining Co. v. Commissioner)

   [For more information on exceptions to capital assets, see Casenote Law Outline on Federal Income Taxation, Chapter 4, § V, Capital Gains and Losses.]

4. **Transactions Related to the Taxpayer.** A taxpayer's motivation in purchasing an asset is irrelevant to the question of whether the asset is "property held by a taxpayer" and is, thus, within I.R.C. § 1221's general definition of a capital asset. (Arkansas Best Corporation v. Commissioner)

   [For more information on capital assets definitions, see Casenote Law Outline on Federal Income Taxation, Chapter 4, § V, Capital Gains and Losses.]

5. **Substitutes for Ordinary Income: Payment for Cancellation of a Lease.** Where the unexpired portion of a lease is settled for cash, the payment received by the taxpayer is merely a substitute for rent and must be reported as ordinary income. (Hort v. Commissioner)

   [For more information on termination payments, see Casenote Law Outline on Federal Income Taxation, Chapter 5, § V, Characterization Issues.]

6. **Substitutes for Ordinary Income: Sale of Interest in a Trust.** A life estate is a capital asset and when disposed of results in capital gains or losses to the life tenant. (McAllister v. Commissioner)

   [For more information on sales of life estates, see Casenote Law Outline on Federal Income Taxation, Chapter 5, § V, Characterization Issues.]

7. **Substitutes for Ordinary Income: Oil Payments.** The transfer of the right to receive future income produces ordinary income to the transfer. (Commissioner v. P. G. Lake, Inc.)

   [For more information on production payments, see Casenote Law Outline on Federal Income Taxation, Chapter 5, § V, Characterization Issues.]

8. **Substitutes for Ordinary Income: Bootstrap Sale to Charity.** Risk-shifting is not essential to a finding that a sale actually occurred. (Commissioner v. Brown)

   [For more information on bootstrap sales, see Casenote Law Outline on Federal Income Taxation, Chapter 5, § V, Characterization Issues.]

9. **Other Claims and Contract Rights: Theatrical Production Rights.** Contract rights said to create in their holder an "estate" in property which, if itself held, would be a capital asset, are themselves capital assets entitled to capital gains treatment. (Commissioner v. Ferrer)

   [For more information on disguised ordinary income, see Casenote Law Outline on Federal Income Taxation, Chapter 4, § V, Capital Gains and Losses.]

10. **Other Claims and Contract Rights: Right of Privacy or of Exploitation.** There is no capitalizable property interest in the image of a public figure which can be passed to another by will or descent. Not everything which can be sold is "property" for tax purposes. (Miller v. Commissioner)

    [For more information on definition of capital asset, see Casenote Law Outline on Federal Income Taxation, Chapter 4, § V, Capital Gains and Losses.]

11. **Bail-Out of Corporate Earnings.** While the motive behind a reorganization is immaterial, the plan must be made pursuant to a legitimate business purpose. (Gregory v. Helvering)

    [For more information on general tax doctrines, see Casenote Law Outline on Federal Income Taxation, Chapter 9, § III, Preventing Assignment of Income and Deductions.]

12. **Fragmentation versus Unification of Collective Assets.** The assets of a business must be separately treated to determine if income from their sales is capital or ordinary based on § 1221. (Williams v. McGowan)

    [For more information on definition of capital gains and losses, see Casenote Law Outline on Federal Income Taxation, Chapter 4, § V, Capital Gains and Losses.]

13. **Correlation with Prior Related Transactions.** When a debt which is deemed worthless is deducted from ordinary income, a subsequent sale or recovery of the debt yields ordinary income. (Merchants National Bank v. Commissioner)

    [For more information on "recapture" rules, see Casenote Law Outline on Federal Income Taxation, Chapter 4, § V, Capital Gains and Losses.]

14. **Correlation with Prior Related Transactions.** A series of related transactions, even though occurring in different tax years, may be considered together in determining the proper classification of the most recent transaction for tax purposes. (Arrowsmith v. Commissioner)

    [For more information on the Arrowsmith doctrine, see Casenote Law Outline on Federal Income Taxation, Chapter 8, § I, The Taxable Year.]

15. **Requirement of a Sale or Exchange.** Losses sustained from the forced sale of a capital asset result in capital losses. (Helvering v. Hammel)

    [For more information on gains from involuntary conversion, see Casenote Law Outline on Federal Income Taxation, Chapter 4, § V, Capital Gains and Losses.]

VAN SUETENDAEL v. COMMISSIONER
Taxpayer (P) v. IRS (D)
3 T.C.M. 987 (1944); aff'd, 152 F.2d 654 (2d Cir. 1945).

NATURE OF CASE: Appeal from Commissioner's (D) determination that the securities sold were capital assets.

FACT SUMMARY: Van Suetendael (P) did some minor investment work as part of his primary activity of trading for his own benefit.

CONCISE RULE OF LAW: Taxpayers who buy securities for speculation or investment hold them as capital assets and not primarily for resale to customers.

FACTS: Van Suetendael (P) was engaged in buying and selling securities. Approximately 90 percent of the securities purchased were interest bearing bonds. Van Suetendael (P) derived most of his income from interest payments. He was not a stock exchange member, but did do some advertising, was listed as a securities dealer and sold some stocks and bonds to others. Assets sold by him were reported as ordinary gains and losses. The Commissioner (D) determined that these were capital assets, denied the ordinary loss deduction and assessed a deficiency. Van Suetendael (P) appealed claiming that the securities were purchased and held primarily for resale to customers.

ISSUE: Where the main thrust of a taxpayer's activities are trading in securities for his own benefit, are securities purchased by him capital assets?

HOLDING AND DECISION: (Harron, J.) Yes. Securities purchased by a "dealer" may be of two types. Bulk wholesale transactions in which the dealer is acting as a middleman come under the exemption in § 1221(1) which excepts property held for sale to customers from being treated as capital assets. However, where the taxpayer buys securities for speculation or investment, they are held as capital assets and not primarily for resale to customers. Van Suetendael (P) was not a middleman. He resold securities to others of the same class as himself, i.e., other investors or speculators. He did not take orders for the purchase of securities, but invested for his own benefit and subsequent resales depended on the nature of the security's activities during the time they were held. Van Suetendael's (P) principal income was derived from investments and interest, not fees from trading. Van Suetendael (P) has not sustained the burden of showing that the securities sold by him were held primarily for resale to customers. Not having sustained this burden, they must be considered capital assets which upon sale yield capital gains and losses. The Commissioner's (D) decision is sustained.

EDITOR'S ANALYSIS: A securities dealer may segregate his accounts so that his personal investment stocks will receive capital gains treatment. Carl Marks and Co. v. Commissioner, 12 T.C. 1196 (1949). Section 1246 requires that these securities must be clearly identified from the start or they will be denied capital gains treatment.

[For more information on capital assets, see Casenote Law Outline on Federal Income Taxation, Chapter 4, § V, Capital Gains and Losses.]

QUICKNOTES

CAPITAL ASSET - Asset, defined in § 1221, the sale or exchange of which produces Capital Gain or Loss.

CAPITAL GAIN AND LOSS - Gain or loss from the "Sale or Exchange" of a "Capital Asset" as defined in § 1221.

NOTES:

BIEDENHARN REALTY CO., INC. v. UNITED STATES

Corporation (P) v. Federal government (D)

526 F.2d 409 (5th Cir.); cert. denied, 429 U.S. 819 (1976).

NATURE OF CASE: Appeal from determination of a tax liability as a capital gain.

FACT SUMMARY: Biedenharn (P) sold subdivisions of its plantation after originally purchasing the plantation for farming, and the Government (D) claimed that the profit on the sales was ordinary income.

CONCISE RULE OF LAW: When dispositions of subdivided property extend over a long period of time and are especially numerous, the likelihood that the profit on such dispositions is a capital gain is very slight.

FACTS: Biedenharn (P), a taxpayer corporation, was formed in 1923 to hold and manage family investments. In 1935, Biedenharn (P) purchased a 973-acre plantation, "Hardtimes," for $50,000. The land was leased for farming and was located near the expanding town of Monroe, La. Between 1939 and 1966, three subdivisions totaling 185 acres were carved out of "Hardtimes." An $800,000 profit was made out of 208 lots sold in 158 sales, and such profit apparently was reported as capital gain prior to 1964-66, the years in question. In a pre-1964 settlement with the Government (D), it was agreed that 60 percent of the gain would be reported as ordinary income and 40 percent as capital gain. Biedenharn (P) reported its 1964-66 earnings in the same manner, and the Government (D) asserted a deficiency, claiming that all earnings were ordinary income. Biedenharn (P) then filed for a refund, claiming all earnings were capital gains. Starting in 1935, Biedenharn (P) made 12 other sales, totaling 275 acres. It improved the plantation subdivisions with electricity, streets, drainage, water, and sewerage for about $200,000. The district court found that "Hardtimes" was bought originally as an investment, that the intent to subdivide did not arise until the town of Monroe began to grow, and that the gains were capital. Before 1964, all sales were unsolicited, while from 1964-66, 75 percent of the sales were induced by independent brokers. The Government (D) appealed, contending that under § 1221 (1) the lots sold in 1964-66 were held primarily for sale in the ordinary course of trade or business.

ISSUE: When dispositions of subdivided property extend over a long period of time and are especially numerous, is the likelihood slight that the profit on such dispositions is capital gain?

HOLDING AND DECISION: (Goldberg, J.) Yes. When dispositions of subdivided property extend over a long period of time and are especially numerous, the likelihood that the profit on such dispositions is a capital gain is very slight. Here, Biedenharn (P) could not claim isolated sales or a passive and gradual liquidation. Even if Biedenharn (P) made no significant acquisitions after "Hardtimes," the purpose, system, and continuity of its efforts easily constituted a business. Furthermore, the business nature of the activity was evidenced by the extensive improvements made to the subdivision land. Biedenharn's (P) failure to advertise did not diminish its business activity because the market was favorable and unsolicited purchasers were buying. While the land sales may have amounted to a modest share of Biedenharn's (P) total profit, Biedenharn (P) made extraordinary profits from stock sales which only diminished the apparent size of the land sale profit on a comparative basis. Thus, it appeared that the land was held for sale in the ordinary course of business and was ordinary income. Reversed.

DISSENT: (Gee, C.J.) "Holding that property is not part of a business only so long as it is sold in large blocks, but not if sold in small parcels, discriminates irrationally against an investor who decides on liquidation but cannot locate purchasers interested in large acquisitions."

EDITOR'S ANALYSIS: Basically, Biedenharn (P) was arguing that its original intent of purchasing the plantation for investment purposes would have been controlling. While it was not controlling here, there can be instances where an initial investment purpose endures in controlling fashion notwithstanding continuing sales activity. Apparently, Congress did not intend to disqualify bona fide investors from capital gains advantages when they are forced to abandon their prior purposes for reasons beyond their control. Such reasons include Acts of God, condemnation of property, unfavorable zoning changes, and physical changes in land.

[For more information on capital gains, see Casenote Law Outline on Federal Income Taxation, Chapter 4, § V, Capital Gains and Losses.]

NOTES:

CORN PRODUCTS REFINING CO. v. COMMISSIONER
Grain products manufacturer (P) v. IRS (D)
350 U.S. 46 (1955).

NATURE OF CASE: Appeal from decision of court of appeals affirming Commissioner's (D) decision that profits and losses from trading in corn futures produced ordinary income and losses.

FACT SUMMARY: Because of corn shortages in the previous year, Corn Products Refinery (P) began to purchase corn futures on the commodities market to protect its supply.

CONCISE RULE OF LAW: Where the purchase of commodity futures is an integral part of a taxpayer's business, it is not a true capital investment, and gains or losses produce ordinary income or losses.

FACTS: Corn Products Refinery (P) found it very difficult to purchase corn because drought conditions forced the price up to a point where its products would be too expensive to compete with other brands. To protect itself, Corn Products (P) began to purchase corn futures. Gains and losses were reported as ordinary income or ordinary losses. After several years, Corn Products (P) claimed that it was really a true capitalistic investor and it was investing in capital assets. Therefore, profits and losses should be treated as capital gains and losses. The Commissioner (D) found that this was not a true capital investment, but was an integral part of Corn Product's (P) business operation. It was designed to hedge against rising price and to provide a ready made source of raw materials.

ISSUE: When a taxpayer's investment in commodity futures is an integral part of its business, should income and losses be treated as ordinary income?

HOLDING AND DECISION: (Clark, J.) Yes. Corn Products (P) contends that it was an investor which purchased a capital asset and should qualify for capital gains treatment. This ignores the realities of the situation. Corn Product's (P) officers testified that the futures were used as a source of supply and as a hedge against rising prices. The company used these futures extensively in its business operations and considered the income and losses as ordinary on its tax returns. This finding was sustained by both the Tax Court and the court of appeals. While commodity futures fit the definition of capital assets contained in § 1221, this section should not be so broadly interpreted as to defeat the reason for Congress' passage of it. It applies to property which is not the source of normal business income and is used to stimulate the economic community by giving tax breaks to investors. Corn Products' (P) use of these futures is not within the meaning of capital assets as envisioned by Congress. Therefore, the decision of the Commissioner (D) is sustained.

EDITOR'S ANALYSIS: In Hollywood Baseball Assoc. v. Commissioner, 423 F.2d 494 (9th Cir. 1970), the players' contracts of a minor league baseball club were found to be within the Corn Products rule. Since the club was required to sell their player contracts to the major clubs on demand, the court found that this was really a sales item pursuant to contract agreements. In effect, these contracts were raw material or stock in trade. Such an item was considered to be integral to the club's business and was treated as producing ordinary income.

[For more information on exceptions to capital assets, see Casenote Law Outline on Federal Income Taxation, Chapter 4, § V, Capital Gains and Losses.]

QUICKNOTES

ASSET - An item or real or personal property that is owned and has tangible value.

CAPITAL GAIN AND LOSS - Gain or loss from the "Sale or Exchange" of a "Capital Asset" as defined in § 1221.

NOTES:

ARKANSAS BEST CORP. v. COMMISSIONER
Stock seller (P) v. IRS (D)
485 U.S. 212 (1988).

NATURE OF CASE: Appeal from disallowance of tax deduction.

FACT SUMMARY: Arkansas Best Co. (P) brought an action against the Commissioner (D) when the Commissioner (D) disallowed Arkansas Best's (P) deduction for an ordinary loss of $9,995,688, resulting from the sale of stock, finding that the loss from the sale was a capital loss and subject to the capital loss limitations in the Internal Revenue Code.

CONCISE RULE OF LAW: A taxpayer's motivation in purchasing an asset is irrelevant to the question of whether the asset is "property held by a taxpayer" and is, thus, within I.R.C. § 1221's general definition of a capital asset.

FACTS: Arkansas Best (P), a diversified holding company, acquired about 65 percent of the stock of National Bank of Commerce. Best (P) more than tripled the number of shares it owned in the bank, although its percentage interest in the bank remained relatively stable. These acquisitions were prompted by the bank's need for added capital. Best (P) sold the bulk of its bank stock after the financial health of the bank declined. On its federal income tax return, Best (P) claimed a deduction for an ordinary loss of $9,995,688, resulting from the sale of the stock. The Commissioner of Internal Revenue (D) disallowed the deduction, finding that the loss from the sale of stock was a capital loss, rather than an ordinary loss, and that, therefore, was subject to the loss limitations in the I.R.C. Best (P) challenged the Commissioner's (D) decision in the Tax Court. The Court found that stock acquired by Best (P) while the bank was financially healthy was acquired for an investment purpose and, therefore, constituted a capital asset, giving rise to a capital loss when sold. The stock acquired after the bank became financially unhealthy was acquired for business purposes and, when sold, was held to be an ordinary loss. The Eighth Circuit Court of Appeals reversed, holding all the stock subject to capital-loss treatment. Best (P) appealed.

ISSUE: Is a taxpayer's motivation in purchasing an asset irrelevant to determining whether the asset is "property held by a taxpayer" and is thus within I.R.C. § 1221's general definition of a capital asset?

HOLDING AND DECISION: (Marshall, J.) Yes. A taxpayer's motivation in purchasing an asset is irrelevant to the question of whether the asset is "property held by a taxpayer" and is, thus, within I.R.C. § 1221's general definition of a capital asset. Section 1221 of the Code defines capital asset broadly, as "property held by the taxpayer (whether or not connected with his trade or business)." Best (P), however, argues that the definition does not include property that is acquired and held for a business purpose. In Best's (P) view, an asset's status as "property" thus turns on the motive behind its acquisition. This motive test, however, is nowhere mentioned in § 1221 and is also in direct conflict with the phrase "whether or not connected with his trade or business." The broad definition of "capital asset" explicitly makes irrelevant any consideration of Best's (P) motives for buying the bank stock whenever it was purchased. As it was an investment, whether or not Best (P) so intended it to be, the shares fell within the broad definition of the term "capital asset" in § 1221. Thus, the loss arising from the sale of the stock was a capital loss. Affirmed.

EDITOR'S ANALYSIS: Capital loss limitations are dealt with in §§ 1211(a) and 1212(a) of the I.R.C. Title 26 U.S.C. § 1211(a) states that in the case of a corporation, losses from sales or exchanges of capital assets shall be allowed only to the extent of gains from such sales or exchanges. Section 1212(a) establishes rules governing carryback and carryovers of capital losses, allowing such losses to offset capital gains in certain earlier or later years.

[For more information on capital assets definitions, see Casenote Law Outline on Federal Income Taxation, Chapter 4, § V, Capital Gains and Losses.]

QUICKNOTES

CAPITAL ASSET - Asset, defined in § 1221, the sale or exchange of which produces Capital Gain or Loss.

CAPITAL GAIN AND LOSS - Gain or loss from the "Sale or Exchange" of a "Capital Asset" as defined in § 1221.

NOTES:

HORT v. COMMISSIONER

Office building owner (P) v. IRS (D)
313 U.S. 28 (1941).

NATURE OF CASE: Appeal from circuit court decision affirming Commissioner's (D) denial of a deduction for the value of the unexpired portion of a lease.

FACT SUMMARY: Hort (P) allowed a lease to be canceled in exchange for $140,000.

CONCISE RULE OF LAW: Where the unexpired portion of a lease is settled for cash, the payment received by the taxpayer is merely a substitute for rent and must be reported as ordinary income.

FACTS: Hort (P) was left a building under the terms of his father's will. One of the tenants, Irving Trust Co., wished to terminate the lease prior to its expiration date. They settled the lease by paying Hort (P) $140,000 in exchange for being released from it. Hort (P) did not report the $140,000 as income and claimed a deduction for the difference between the fair-rental value of the space for the unexpired term of the lease and the $140,000 he received. The Commissioner (D) disallowed the deduction and assessed a deficiency tax on the $140,000. Hort (P) claimed that the $140,000 was a capital gain and even if it was ordinary income he sustained a loss on the unexpired portion of the lease. The Tax Court and the circuit court sustained the Commissioner.

ISSUE: Where a lease is terminated prior to the expiration date and the taxpayer receives cash compensation, must it be reported as ordinary income?

HOLDING AND DECISION: (Murphy, J.) Yes. Hort (P) received the money, after negotiations, as a substitute for rent. Section 61(a) would have required Hort (P) to include prepaid rent or an award for breach of contract as income. Hort (P) received an amount of money in lieu of the rental income he was entitled to under the lease. Since it was a substitute for ordinary income, it must be treated in the same manner. The consideration received by Hort (P) was not a return of capital. A lease is not considered a capital asset within the context of § 61(a). Further, the fact that Hort (P) received less than he would have under the terms of the lease does not entitle him to a deduction. No loss was sustained. He released a legal right for a settlement sum. Hort (P) didn't have to do so, and having made the decision to settle the amount realized by him must be deemed fair. Any injury to Hort (P) can only be fixed when the extent of the loss can be ascertained, i.e., when the property is re-rented. Until that time, no loss is deductible. The decision of the Commissioner (D) is sustained.

EDITOR'S ANALYSIS: In U.S. v. Dresser Industries, Inc., 324 F.2d 56 (5th Cir. 1963), the Court addressed itself to the "anticipated future income" problem. The Court held that the only commercial value of any property is the present worth of future earnings or usefulness. If the government can challenge a sale based on the fact that the sales price is only a substitute for future earnings, then no asset could qualify for capital gains treatment. The question of capital gains treatment really revolves around whether the present sale represents the right to "earn" future income or the right to "earned" future income.

[For more information on termination payments, see Casenote Law Outline on Federal Income Taxation, Chapter 5, § V, Characterization Issues.]

QUICKNOTES

CAPITAL ASSET - Asset, defined in § 1221, the sale or exchange of which produces Capital Gain or Loss.

CAPITAL GAIN AND LOSS - Gain or loss from the "Sale or Exchange" of a "Capital Asset" as defined in § 1221.

GROSS INCOME - The total income earned by an individual or business.

LOSS - Situation where Amount realized (if any) exceeds the basis upon the sale or other disposition of an asset. Also refers to fact of "Sustained" decline in value of asset (not disposed of) which gives rise to a deduction. There is also said to be a loss in a year where deductions exceed gross income.

NOTES:

McALLISTER v. COMMISSIONER

Taxpayer (P) v. IRS (D)

157 F.2d 235 (2d Cir. 1946); cert. denied, 330 U.S. 826 (1947).

NATURE OF CASE: Appeal from decision of Tax Court affirming Commissioner's (D) decision that money received for the release of a life estate is ordinary income.

FACT SUMMARY: In order to terminate a trust, the remainderman paid McAllister (P) $55,000 to release her life estate.

CONCISE RULE OF LAW: A life estate is a capital asset and when disposed of results in capital gains or losses to the life tenant.

FACTS: McAllister (P) had a life estate in the income from a trust. In order to meet expenses, she sold her life estate to the remainderman for $55,000. This was approximately $8,800 less than the actuarial value of the life estate discounted to present worth. She attempted to deduct this amount as a capital loss. The Commissioner (D) found that this "sale" was merely the advance receipt of income and should be taxed accordingly. The Tax Court affirmed.

ISSUE: Is a life estate a capital asset which will result in capital gains or loss treatment when it is sold?

HOLDING AND DECISION: (Clark, J.) Yes. McAllister's (P) right to income for life from the trust was a right in the estate itself. The transfer of a substantial life estate is a disposition of a capital asset. McAllister (P) assigned her interest in the estate as well as her right to receive income. The release signed by her relinquished all rights she had in the trust. The decision in the Hort case may be distinguished in two respects. First, there is a difference between a lease and a substantial life estate. Secondly, there is a very real difference in the release of a contract right to receive income for a reasonably short time and the total transfer of a substantial property right such as a life estate. For these reasons, the decision of the Commissioner (D) is overruled.

DISSENT: (Frank, J.) This type of transaction does not fall within the parameters of § 1221. Congress never intended to grant capital gains treatment in this situation. McAllister (P) had the right to receive income during her lifetime. She had no interest in the corpus. Yearly payments to her would be considered ordinary income. The "sale" of the life estate was no different than an advance payment of dividends, income, or interest. It is doubtful that Congress intended to change such payments into capital gains or losses.

EDITOR'S ANALYSIS: In Bell v. Harrison, 212 F.2d 253 (7th Cir. 1954), the court held that a remainderman who purchased the life tenant's interest could amortize his cost over the expected duration of the life estate. While the purchase was of a capital asset, the court rejected the concept that the life estate merged with the remainder after purchase.

[For more information on sales of life estates, see Casenote Law Outline on Federal Income Taxation, Chapter 5, § V, Characterization Issues.]

QUICKNOTES

LIFE ESTATE - An interest in land measured by the life of the tenant or a third party.

REMAINDERMAN - A person who has an interest in property to commence upon the termination of a present possessory interest.

NOTES:

COMMISSIONER v. P.G. LAKE, INC.
IRS (D) v. Taxpayers (P)
356 U.S. 260 (1958).

NATURE OF CASE: Appeal by Commissioner (D) from court of appeals decision finding that an assignment of mineral payment rights produces capital gains to the assignor.

FACT SUMMARY: Lake (P) assigned a portion of its rights to oil payments to its president in exchange for his cancellation of a debt owed to him by the corporation.

CONCISE RULE OF LAW: The transfer of the right to receive future income produces ordinary income to the transfer.

FACTS: Five cases are consolidated herein. They involve a common question. If a taxpayer assigns a portion of his right to receive mineral payments to another in exchange for money or other property, how is the transaction treated? In the Lake case, the president of Lake (P) agreed to cancel a $600,000 debt if Lake (P) would assign a portion of its oil payment rights to him. Lake Corp. (P) did so, and attempted to report the $600,000 forgiveness as capital gains. The Commissioner (D) held that this was really ordinary income, subject to depletion. An additional question is presented in the Fleming case. The assignment was made for land rather than cash, but the Commissioner (D) held that this was not an exchange of like capital assets so as to postpone realization.

ISSUE: Is the right to receive mineral payments a capital asset which when assigned would produce capital gains?

HOLDING AND DECISION: No. While the right to receive oil payments is an interest in property, Congress could not have intended this type of transaction to qualify for special treatment. First, there has been no conversion of a capital asset. The companies involved here merely assigned for a relatively short period of time their right to receive income. The pay out on these leases could be measured with considerable accuracy so the sale must be deemed a closed transaction. The lump sum considerations for these assignments were essentially a substitute for future income payments. What was paid for was the right to receive payments from these oil rights. Nothing was being paid for any increase in the value of a capital asset. For these reasons, the income received by these corporations must be considered as ordinary income, subject to depletion. In the Fleming case, we agree with the court of appeals that an exchange of land for the right to receive future income is not an exchange of like capital assets. The Commissioner's (D) decision in all of these cases is sustained.

EDITOR'S ANALYSIS: A careful reading of Lake would seem to indicate that this decision overrules McAllister v. Commissioner, 157 F.2d 235 (2d Cir. 1946). However, McAllister may be distinguished on the basis that she actually transferred all of her

rights in the life estate, while in Lake the assignment was only partial. Also Lake's (P) interest was in receiving future payments rather than the more substantial property right possessed by McAllister.

[For more information on production payments, see Casenote Law Outline on Federal Income Taxation, Chapter 5, § V, Characterization Issues.]

QUICKNOTES

ASSIGNMENT - A transaction in which a party conveys his or her entire interest in property to another.

REALIZATION - General principle under which gains and losses are deemed to "exist" for income tax purposes only when "realized," referring to some event which marks the taxpayer's change of status with respect to the asset, principally as the result of sale, exchange, or disposition. A "deemed realization rule" is one wherein the tax law treats a nonrealization event as a realization event.

NOTES:

COMMISSIONER v. BROWN
IRS (D) v. Lumber mill owners (P)
380 U.S. 563 (1965).

NATURE OF CASE: Appeal by Commissioner (D) from adverse decision of Tax Court and court of appeals that the sale of a business resulted in a capital gain.

FACT SUMMARY: The Institute of Cancer Research purchased a lumber company from Brown (P) for a small amount of money and long-term notes.

CONCISE RULE OF LAW: Risk-shifting is not essential to a finding that a sale actually occurred.

FACTS: Clay Brown (P) and other members of his family owned a sawmill and lumber. The California Institute of Cancer Research approached him with an offer to purchase the company. It was agreed that the stock should be sold for $1.3 million, payable $5,000 down from the company's assets and the balance over a 10-year period from its profits. Simultaneous to the transaction, the company's assets were to be liquidated and a new corporation, Fortuna Sawmills, Inc., was to be established. Fortuna was to lease the assets of the liquidated company for 5 years. Fortuna would pay 80 percent of its profits to the Institute, a tax-exempt organization, which would then pay 90 percent of this amount to Clay Brown (P) and the other shareholders as payment of these notes. Brown (P) was given a management contract with Fortuna. Four years later, Fortuna closed down due to economic losses. The notes provided that the Institute had no personal liability and if payments failed to total $250,000 over a two-year period, Brown (P) could accelerate the notes. Fortuna was sold by the Institute which retained 10 percent of the proceeds. The rest was applied to the notes. Total payments received by Brown (P) and the others was $936,131. The Commissioner (D) determined that these payments were ordinary income. Brown (P) appealed and was affirmed by both the Tax Court and court of appeals on the basis that this was a real sale and not a sham transaction.

ISSUE: Where a purchaser invests nothing in a business and has no personal liability for payments of the purchase price, has a legitimate sale taken place?

HOLDING AND DECISION: Yes. The price paid for the stock was fair. It was within a reasonable range based on the corporation's past performance. The price was negotiated through arms-length bargaining. The sale of a capital asset yields capital gains/losses. If payments are made on the installment basis under § 453, taxes are only imposed as the installments are received. The fact that the Institute paid no money for the business and assumed no personal risk for the repayment of the obligation is immaterial. Likewise, the retention of Brown (P) and the lack of control over the business' operation do not indicate a sham transaction. The "sale" was not a subterfuge. The Tax Court found that it was made for fair value and was a legitimate transaction. The Commissioner (D) has been unable to demonstrate otherwise. The Commissioner (D) ignores the fact that if the rents payable by Fortuna were deductible by it and the Institute was not taxed on them, the purchase price could be paid off at a far more rapid rate. This is of considerable importance to a seller who wants his money as rapidly as possible. Since risk-shifting is not, by itself, a material factor and Congress has not held that the retention, by the seller, of an interest in capital assets would disqualify the transaction, the decision of the court of appeals must be affirmed.

CONCURRENCE: (Harlan, J.) The tax laws are a reality which businessmen must live with. There is no prohibition associated with taking advantage of the favorable tax treatment accorded to charities. Had the Government argued that the transaction should be divided into a transfer of assets and the right to future income, and that only the latter should be accorded capital gains treatment, the decision must have been different.

DISSENT: (Goldberg, J.) By countenancing this type of transaction, the majority has allowed the taxpayers to receive the income of the corporation, up to $131,000, at capital gains rates. Since no economic risk-shifting occurred, and since all payments were to be made out of ordinary income, the transaction should not be given favorable capital gains treatment.

EDITOR'S ANALYSIS: In TIR 768, Oct. 5, 1965, 65-7 CCH St. and Fed. Tax Rep. § 6739; Rev. Rul. 66-153, 1966-1 C.B. 187, the Commissioner stated that henceforth, he would only attack transactions where the purchase price was excessive. In 1969, § 514 was amended to make debt-financed income taxable to nonprofit and charitable organizations.

[For more information on bootstrap sales, see ***Casenote Law Outline on Federal Income Taxation,*** *Chapter 5, § V, Characterization Issues.]*

MILLER v. COMMISSIONER
Taxpayer (P) v. IRS (D)
299 F.2d 706 (2d Cir.); cert. denied, 370 U.S. 923 (1962).

NATURE OF CASE: Appeal from Commissioner's (D) decision that the proceeds from the sale of an asset produced ordinary income.

FACT SUMMARY: Mrs. Miller (P) sold Universal Pictures the right to make a picture concerning the life of her husband, Glenn Miller.

CONCISE RULE OF LAW: There is no capitalizable property interest in the image of a public figure which can be passed to another by will or descent. Not everything which can be sold is "property" for tax purposes.

FACTS: Mrs. Miller (P) entered into a contract with Universal Pictures in connection with its filming "The Glenn Miller Story." Miller (P) granted Universal the exclusive right to produce, release, and exhibit theatrical ventures based on the life of her husband. Miller (P) was to be granted royalty payments. Miller (P) claimed that these payments represented capital gains from the sale or exchange of a capital asset held over six months. The Commissioner (D) held that this was not "property" capable of being given special tax treatment and determined that it should be taxed as ordinary income.

ISSUE: Is the sale of another's public image a capital asset upon which capital gains may be realized?

HOLDING AND DECISION: (Kaufman, J.) No. First, Mrs. Miller (P) did not possess a "property" interest in her deceased husband's image. Many things can be sold which are not "property," *e.g.*, one's time and experience. It does not appear that under current law Universal could have been sued by Mrs. Miller (P) if it had produced the picture without her consent. The fact that Universal preferred to "pay her off" to avoid potential litigation or future charges in the law does not elevate Mrs. Miller's (P) interest to a "property right." We do not believe that even if this were a property right it should be given preferential tax treatment. The congressional purpose for granting favorable capital gains treatment is to relieve taxpayers from excessive tax burdens on the conversion of certain assets. This purpose would not be furthered by granting beneficiaries of a decedent a capitalizable "property" interest in the name, reputation, etc. of the deceased. The Commissioner's (D) decision is affirmed.

EDITOR'S ANALYSIS: See also Kunyon v. United States, 281 F.2d 590 (5th Cir. 1960), holding that the right to privacy is not a capital asset. Further, Rev. Rul. 65-261, 1965-2 C.B. 281, held that the sale of exclusive and perpetual rights to the commercial exploitation of the name of a famous individual is not a capital asset. The value of Miller's name and image may have had great potential value. Advertising endorsements provide personalities with a large amount of income. In other areas of the law, the unauthorized use of one's name or image is actionable as an infringement on a property right. Evidently, the court was unwilling to recognize this as a descendible right and/or to afford it capital gains treatment.

[For more information on definition of capital asset, see Casenote Law Outline on Federal Income Taxation, Chapter 4, § V, Capital Gains and Losses.]

NOTES:

COMMISSIONER v. FERRER
IRS (P) v. Stage producer (D)
304 F.2d 125 (2d Cir. 1962).

NATURE OF CASE: Decision of Tax Court holding taxpayer not liable for alleged tax deficiencies is appealed by the Commissioner of the Internal Revenue Service.

FACT SUMMARY: Ferrer (D) sold his rights under a contract for the production of a play in exchange for certain benefits he derived under a contract for the production of a movie. Ferrer (D) characterized his gains from the sale as capital gains a characterization with which the Commissioner (P) disagreed. Although Ferrer (D) prevailed in the Tax Court, the Commissioner (P) is appealing herein.

CONCISE RULE OF LAW: Contract rights said to create in their holder an "estate" in property which, if itself held, would be a capital asset, are themselves capital assets entitled to capital gains treatment.

FACTS: Jose Ferrer (D) entered into an elaborate contractual arrangement with Pierre LaMure, author of the novel, "Moulin Rouge," whereby Ferrer (D) would oversee the production of the stage version of the work. First, LaMure "leased" to Ferrer "the sole and exclusive right" to produce and present the play on stage in the U.S. and Canada. Second, the contract, entered into November 1, 1951, gave Ferrer (D) the right, incident to the lease, to prevent any disposition of the motion picture rights until June 1, 1952, or, on making an additional $1,500 advance, to December 1, 1952, and for a period thereafter if he produced the play, and to prevent disposition of the radio and television rights even longer. Third, if Ferrer produced the play, he was entitled to 40 percent of all proceeds of the motion picture and other rights. Pierre LaMure was to receive specified royalties on all box office receipts. Shortly after the above contract was signed, Ferrer (D) was approached by a Mr. John Huston, representing what was to become Moulin Productions Inc., who asked to purchase the motion picture rights to "Moulin Rouge." Under a contract between Ferrer (D) and Moulin Productions Inc., Ferrer (D) sold the rights he had acquired under the dramatic production contract. Ferrer (D) characterized the full amount he received from the sale of his rights as capital gains. The Commissioner (P) sued on the theory the amounts received were ordinary income.

ISSUE: Are contract rights which give their holder an "estate" in property which is itself a capital asset, themselves entitled to capital gains treatment upon their sale or exchange as capital assets?

HOLDING AND DECISION: (Friendly, J.) Yes. It is extremely difficult to formulate a general rule for the identification of capital assets. However, in reviewing the authority in this area, one common characteristic of the cases holding property to be capital assets can be isolated: the taxpayer in each case had either what might be called an "estate" in, or an "encumbrance" on, or an option to acquire an interest in property which, if itself held, would be a capital asset. Restated, the taxpayer had something more than an opportunity to obtain some benefit afforded by contract. In this case, we are confronted with the sale of three rights afforded the seller, Ferrer (D), by his dramatic production contract. Each of the three rights must be considered separately to determine the character of the gain from its sale as capital or ordinary. First is Ferrer's (D) "lease" of the play. Since a court would have enjoined any interference with Ferrer's (D) exclusive right, it can be said the contract afforded Ferrer (D) an "equitable interest" in the copyright of the play. This "equitable interest" is the "estate" in property (the copyright), which if itself held would be a capital asset. The gain from the sale of the "lease" was, therefore, entitled to capital gains treatment. Second, is Ferrer's (D) negative power to prevent any disposition of the motion picture, radio, and television rights until production of the play. Since equity would also protect this right, Ferrer (D) had an "estate" in the copyright which is itself a capital asset. Under our rule, an "estate" created by contract on property which, if itself held, would be a capital asset, is itself a capital asset, the gain from the sale of which is entitled to capital gains tax treatment. Third, is Ferrer's (D) right to receive 40 percent of the proceeds of the motion picture if he produced the play. Under the dramatic production contract, Ferrer (D) was to "have no right, title or interest, legal or equitable, in the motion picture rights, other than the right to receive" his designated "share of the proceeds." The copyright owner, LaMure, reserved the entire property, both legal and equitable, in himself. Hence, if Ferrer (D) had produced the play and LaMure had sold the motion picture rights, Ferrer's (D) 40 percent of the profits would have been ordinary income. Ferrer (D) merely sold these rights in a lump sum and such a sale cannot change their character from ordinary to capital. The taxpayer, therefore, properly claimed capital gains treatment as to items one and two, while the Commissioner properly challenged the capital gains treatment of item three. The case is remanded for a determination of what percentages of the gains reported fall within each of the three categories discussed.

EDITOR'S ANALYSIS: Prior to this decision, cancellation of contract rights cases in the Second Circuit were denied capital gains treatment for want of the statutorily required "sale or exchange." In shifting to the analysis in this case of the nature of the rights transferred, rather than the method of transfer, the court has moved away from the basic policies of capital gains taxation, *i.e.*, that capital gains treatment only be afforded situations involving the realization of appreciation on value accrued over a substantial period of time. An analysis focusing on the method of transfer rather than the nature of the rights transferred better serves this ultimate purpose.

GREGORY v. HELVERING
Sale shareholder (P) v. IRS (D)
293 U.S. 465 (1935).

NATURE OF CASE: Appeal from reversal of Tax Board's decision denying the Commissioner's delinquent tax assessment.

FACT SUMMARY: Gregory (P) attempted to funnel shares of stock from one corporation to another under the guise of a "reorganization."

CONCISE RULE OF LAW: While the motive behind a reorganization is immaterial, the plan must be made pursuant to a legitimate business purpose.

FACTS: Gregory (P) was the sole shareholder of United Mortgage Corp. United held 1,000 shares of Monitor Securities Corp. Gregory (P), in an attempt to personally own these shares, formed a new corporation. Gregory (P) then had these shares transferred to the new corporation pursuant to a plan of reorganization under § 112 of the Internal Revenue Code. Gregory then dissolved the new corporation, and as sole shareholder, received the stocks which were the corporation's sole assets. Gregory (P) then sold the shares and paid only a capital gains tax on the proceeds. The Commissioner assessed a delinquent tax on the sale claiming that this was, in reality, a dividend and should be treated as ordinary income. The Tax Board of Appeals overruled the Commissioner, but was reversed by the court of appeals. Certiorari was granted.

ISSUE: Is a legitimate business purpose required to affect a tax-free reorganization?

HOLDING AND DECISION: (Sutherland, J.) Yes. Gregory (P) does not deny that this was a mere sham transaction to allow her to qualify for a more favorable rate of taxation. Gregory (P) followed the requisites of § 112. A new corporation was formed, assets were transferred, no stock was given up, and Gregory (P) as sole shareholder was in control of both corporations. While a tax avoidance motive is immaterial and may not be looked into, it is necessary to inquire into the purpose of § 112. The purpose was to allow tax-free reorganizations founded on valid business reasons. Since there are no business reasons for these transactions, § 112 does not apply and the income received by Gregory (P) should be treated as a dividend, and taxed as ordinary income.

EDITOR'S ANALYSIS: The above is an example of the court's placing substance over form. In many cases the court will require more than a literal compliance with the statute. In 1954, § 355 was enacted to put all divisive reorganizations on a par, regardless of the form used. A legitimate business purpose must exist to avoid taxation.

MERCHANTS NATIONAL BANK v. COMMISSIONER
Bank (P) v. IRS (D)
199 F.2d 657 (5th Cir. 1952).

NATURE OF CASE: Appeal from Tax Court decision sustaining the Commissioner's (D) determination that income from the sale of notes was ordinary.

FACT SUMMARY: After fully deducting "worthless" notes as ordinary losses, Merchants National Bank (P) was able to sell them to another.

CONCISE RULE OF LAW: When a debt which is deemed worthless is deducted from ordinary income, a subsequent sale or recovery of the debt yields ordinary income.

FACTS: Merchants National Bank (P) determined that notes which it held were worthless. Merchants National Bank (P) charged them off as bad debts and deducted them from its ordinary income. Several years later the Bank (P) was able to sell these notes for $18,460. It attempted to report this income as long-term capital gains. The Commissioner (D) determined that this was ordinary income, and on appeal, the Tax Court affirmed.

ISSUE: Is the sale of a previously charged off asset, the disposition of a capital asset which should yield capital gains income?

HOLDING AND DECISION: (Kaufman, J.) No. The notes had previously been deducted from ordinary income. Merchants National Bank (P) was able to receive maximum deductions by claiming the debt as an ordinary loss. To allow Merchants (P) to now obtain further tax advantages by now claiming capital gains treatment for its subsequent sale is not contemplated under the tax laws. It is well settled that when a deduction is taken and allowed for debts deemed worthless, recoveries on the debt in later years constitute taxable income for that year to the extent of the tax benefit received in the earlier year. The fact that the bank sold the notes rather than collected on them from the debtor cannot avoid the above stated rule. The Commissioner's (D) decision is sustained.

EDITOR'S ANALYSIS: Mitchell v. Commissioner, 428 F.2d 259 (6th Cir. 1970), held that where stock is sold and produces capital gains, a later repayment of the profits, due to a holding that the gain was made with "inside" information, will result in a capital loss deduction. Sections 1251 and 1252 require the recapture of certain farm losses and depreciation as ordinary income. Sections 1245 and 1250 require recapture of income from the sale of previously depreciated property.

[For more information on "recapture" rules, see Casenote Law Outline on Federal Income Taxation, Chapter 4, § V, Capital Gains and Losses.]

WILLIAMS v. McGOWAN
Business partner (P) v. IRS (D)
152 F.2d 570 (2d Cir. 1945).

NATURE OF CASE: Appeal by taxpayer from dismissal of action to recover taxes paid.

FACT SUMMARY: Williams (P) sold his business after buying out his deceased partner's interest in it.

CONCISE RULE OF LAW: The assets of a business must be separately treated to determine if income from their sales is capital or ordinary based on § 1221.

FACTS: Williams (P) and Reynolds formed a partnership. When Reynolds died, Williams (P) purchased Reynolds' interest from the estate. Williams (P) then sold the assets of the business to a third party. Williams (P) reported the sale as an ordinary loss on his tax return. The Commissioner (D) determined that the business was a capital asset which demanded capital gains treatment. William's (P) complaint to recover income taxes paid was dismissed, and he appealed.

ISSUE: Does the sale of a sole proprietorship result in capital gains and losses?

HOLDING AND DECISION: (Learned Hand, J.) No. The assets of a business must be separately treated to determine if income from their sales is capital or ordinary based on § 1221. While it has been held that a partner's interest in a going concern should he treated as a capital asset, when Williams (P) bought Reynolds' share, the business became a sole proprietorship. There is no suggestion of a tax avoidance scheme, and the business must be treated as a sole proprietorship. Since there is no special treatment designated for a sole proprietorship, the court must examine § 1221 in order to determine the appropriate tax treatment. Section 1221 requires that all assets be treated as capital ones unless they fit within three exceptions, *i.e.* stock in trade, property held primarily for resale to customers, or depreciable business property. Williams (P) transferred cash, receivables, fixtures, and inventory. Fixtures are depreciable, and inventory is primarily held for customer resale. Therefore neither of these assets is subject to capital gains treatment. Cash transfers cannot result in gains or losses. Therefore, the only asset that might be deemed capital in nature is the receivables. However, it has not been argued whether they are subject to depreciation. Therefore, the case is remanded to the district court for a decision on this point. All other assets should be treated as yielding ordinary income. Reversed.

DISSENT: (Frank, J.) The parties, in their contract, stated that Williams (P) was to transfer his "rights, title and interest . . . in, and to, the hardware business." Congress did not intend to carve the sale of a business into separate distinct sales. The parties transacted for the sale and purchase of the business as a whole. There does not seem to be any rationale to support the majority's decision either on a contract theory or on the purpose of § 1221. What was sold was the business, not the individual assets.

EDITOR'S ANALYSIS: Good will is considered a capital asset when a business is sold. Rev. Rul. 57-480, 1957-2 C.B. 47; Regs. § 1.167(a)-3. On the other hand, accounts receivable acquired on the sale of inventory property will be deemed non-capital assets, § 1221(4). Since most businesses are on the accrual basis, the receivables will already have been reported as income so § 1221(4) will have little effect on them. It may be more significant for cash basis taxpayers.

[For more information on definition of capital gains and losses, see Casenote Law Outline on Federal Income Taxation, Chapter 4, § V, Capital Gains and Losses.]

QUICKNOTES
CAPITAL GAIN AND LOSS - Gain or loss from the "Sale or Exchange" of a "Capital Asset" as defined in § 1221.

DEPRECIATION - An amount given to a taxpayer as an offset to gross income, to account for the reduction in value of the taxpayer's income producing property due to everyday usage.

SOLE PROPRIETORSHIP - A business owned by an individual and not considered a separate entity for tax purposes; tax liability is incurred on behalf of the business by the owner.

NOTES:

ARROWSMITH v. COMMISSIONER
Shareholder (P) v. IRS (D)
344 U.S. 6 (1952).

NATURE OF CASE: Appeal from decision of court of appeals affirming determination that payment of a judgment yielded capital losses.

FACT SUMMARY: After the assets of a corporation had been liquidated, the transferees of the assets were forced to pay a judgment rendered against the liquidated corporation.

CONCISE RULE OF LAW: A series of related transactions, even though occurring in different tax years, may be considered together in determining the proper classification of the most recent transaction for tax purposes.

FACTS: Arrowsmith (P) and another taxpayer held all the stock in a corporation. The corporation was liquidated over a four-year period. Arrowsmith (P) reported all gains on the transaction as capital gains. Several years after the liquidation, a judgment was rendered against the corporation, and Arrowsmith (P) as one of the transferees of corporate assets had to pay his share of the judgment under § 6901(a)(A). Arrowsmith (P) deducted these payments from his income as ordinary losses. The Commissioner (D) integrated all of the transactions and determined that the payments represented capital losses. The court of appeals affirmed. The Supreme Court granted review.

ISSUE: May related transactions be integrated in order to classify one of them for tax purposes?

HOLDING AND DECISION: (Black, J.) Yes. Arrowsmith (P) correctly states the rule that each year is a separate unit for tax accounting purposes. However, examining related transactions to classify the latest transaction is not an attempt to reopen or readjust earlier tax years. Arrowsmith (P) received capital gain benefits from the corporate distributors. If the judgment had been rendered earlier, it would have reduced the amount of profits available to Arrowsmith (P). By integrating the transactions, it is apparent that Arrowsmith (P) should not receive both favorable capital gains treatment on the original distribution and favorable ordinary loss treatment on the later payment of the judgment. The Commissioner's (D) decision is affirmed.

DISSENT: (Douglas, J.) There were no capital transactions in the year in which the losses were suffered. Those transactions occurred and were accounted for in previous years in accord with the principle that each year is a separate unit for tax acounting purposes.

DISSENT: (Jackson, J.) Congress has not allowed previous tax years to be reopened under these circumstances. The majority is attempting to accomplish a similar result through an integration of all transactions. Without Congressional authorization, this would not appear to be permitted. Second, while treating the judgment payment as ordinary losses may result in a windfall to taxpayers because of the favorable tax rates, the alternative may be equally unfair. Arrowsmith (P) may not be able to fully utilize the capital loss based on the limitation of deductibility. Finally, had the liability been paid by the corporation, it would have been allowed to deduct these payments from its taxes as ordinary losses. This would have resulted in Arrowsmith (P) receiving a greater amount than he will now receive under the majority's reasoning. Solicitude for revenues is a treacherous basis upon which to decide a case. Where the statute is indecisive and the importance of a holding lies in its rational and harmonious relation to the general tax scheme, Great deference should be accorded to previous decisions of the Tax Court which ruled against the Commissioner.

EDITOR'S ANALYSIS: In Werner v. Commissioner, 242 F.2d 938 (9th Cir. 1957), two partners sold their interest for cash and notes. They suffered a loss on the sale. When the notes were later settled for less than their full value, the additional loss sustained by the partners was treated as a long term capital loss under Arrowsmith. In Estate of Shannonhouse v. Commissioner, 54 T.C. 827 (1960), a taxpayer who had sold a parcel of land by warranty deed three years earlier had to pay the purchaser $3,000 because a building on the land encroached on the land of another. The court held that the payment represented a capital loss because it was sustained under the terms of the original capital transaction.

[For more information on the Arrowsmith doctrine, see Casenote Law Outline on Federal Income Taxation, Chapter 8, § I, The Taxable Year.]

QUICKNOTES

CAPITAL GAIN AND LOSS - Gain or loss from the "Sale or Exchange" of a "Capital Asset" as defined in § 1221.

LOSS - Situation where amount realized (if any) exceeds the basis upon the sale or other disposition of an asset. Also refers to fact of "sustained" decline in value of asset (not disposed of) which gives rise to a deduction. There is also said to be a loss in a year where deductions exceed gross income.

HELVERING v. HAMMEL
Syndicate member (P) v. IRS (D)
311 U.S. 504 (1941).

NATURE OF CASE: Appeal by Commissioner (D) from a decision by the circuit court which overruled his determination that a loss was capital in nature.

FACT SUMMARY: A syndicate purchased land for development purposes on a land contract, but later lost it when payments were defaulted on by them.

CONCISE RULE OF LAW: Losses sustained from the forced sale of a capital asset result in capital losses.

FACTS: Hammel (P) was the member of a syndicate which purchased land for development purposes. The purchase was made under a land sale contract. When the syndicate defaulted on payments, the vendor instituted foreclosure proceedings which resulted in a judicial sale of the property and a deficiency judgment against the syndicate members. Hammel's (P) share of these losses was $4,000 which he attempted to claim as an ordinary loss deduction. The Commissioner (D) disallowed the deduction claiming that this was a capital loss resulting from the sale or exchange of a capital asset. Hammel (P) argued that § 1211(b) which provides for capital loss treatment from the sale or exchange of a capital asset does not apply to a forced sale. Rather, § 165(c)(2) should apply which would allow him to deduct the entire loss from ordinary income. The circuit court supported Hammel's (P) contention and overruled the Commissioner (D).

ISSUE: Will the forced sale of a capital asset yield ordinary income?

HOLDING AND DECISION: (Stone, J.) No. Section 117 of the Code provides that capital losses in excess of capital gains may only be deducted from ordinary income up to $2,000. Congress specifically limited the amount of loss which might be deducted from ordinary income when a capital asset is sold. Without some clear legislative statement that this treatment is not to apply to the forced sale of capital assets, we must follow this specific statutory mandate. Hammel (P) cannot prevail with his argument that this was not a sale or exchange within the meaning of § 1211. While the land was ordered sold by the court, the definitive act severing all of the syndicate's rights was the actual sale of the property. This qualifies as a "sale or exchange" unless specifically exempted by Congress. For these reasons, the Commissioner's (D) denial of the ordinary deduction is sustained.

EDITOR'S ANALYSIS: Section 1231 now makes the destruction of an asset and the subsequent compensation by insurance a sale or exchange. Where the sale is not a "closed" transaction no tax is imposed and no loss is recognized. Therefore, Rev. Rul. 70-63 prescribes that a tax sale will not be considered a closed transaction where the taxpayer has a right of redemption, therefore, no loss deduction will be allowed until the redemption period is expired.

[For more information on gains from involuntary conversion, see Casenote Law Outline on Federal Income Taxation, Chapter 4, § V, Capital Gains and Losses.]

QUICKNOTES

CAPITAL ASSET - Asset, defined in § 1221, the sale or exchange of which produces Capital Gain or Loss.

NOTES: